Your Well-Being Garden

Your Well-Being Garden

HOW TO MAKE YOUR GARDEN GOOD FOR YOU

SCIENCE | DESIGN | PRACTICE

ALISTAIR GRIFFITHS
MATT KEIGHTLEY

ANNIE GATTI
ZIA ALLAWAY

Contents

The Protective Garden

The Healing Garden

The Nourishing Garden

The Sustainable Garden

Your garden can heal...

Monty Don

Writer, gardener, and TV presenter

 I know from personal experience how gardening helps heal many mental and physical ills. When you are sad, a garden comforts. When you are humiliated or defeated, a garden consoles. When you are consumed by anxiety, it will soothe you, and when the world is a dark and bleak place, it shines a light to guide you on.

Alice Vincent

Journalist and author

 Your Well-Being Garden is that rare thing: a book that will make gardeners out of people who didn't know they could be. With ideas for every kind of outdoor space, this book beautifully explains how to improve the world around us in a way that—crucially—makes us feel better.

James Wong

Botanist, science writer, and broadcaster

Both as a plant scientist and a home gardener, I am a passionate believer in the therapeutic power of plants. Professor Alistair Griffiths has brilliantly summed up the most cutting-edge research in this field in such a readable, relatable way, I am now his biggest fan. And after this book, I reckon there'll be a queue!

Ellen Mary

Presenter, writer, and gardener

When I spend time outside, I instinctively feel a natural shift allowing me to tune in with everything around—from birdsong, worms working the soil, and watching plants bloom, to the changing seasons. Touching the soil, sowing seeds, and nurturing growth isn't just about reconnecting with nature, it's about 'remembering' that we *are* nature. This mindful process is so good for our well-being. When that realization happens, you can view the world in a whole new way, and gardening allows that to happen every day.

Preface

We are at an exciting time, for both gardens and people. There is an ever-increasing body of scientific evidence that gardens and gardening are good for our physical, mental, and social well-being.

A gardening green revolution has started, highlighting the critical importance of gardens to human well-being. There are very few, if any, other activities that can achieve all of the things that horticulture and gardening can—in particular, the measurable impact on active lifestyles, mental well-being, and social interaction.

Gardening helps us to keep fit and to connect with others, to enjoy and be part of nature, and to revel in color, wildlife, and beauty. Simply contemplating nature helps to rest and recharge our brains. Aside from cultivating beautiful plants that delight our senses, we can also grow food and even cures for minor ailments in our green spaces. Gardens and plants also improve our environment, protecting us from noise and pollution, as well as extremes of temperature.

Scientific research led by the Royal Horticultural Society (RHS) continues to improve and share understanding on how to maximize gardening's benefits—to both human health and the environment. For the past few years, the RHS Science Team— primarily based at RHS Garden Wisley, Surrey— together with colleagues from several UK, European,

and US universities, has been looking at how garden plants, gardens, and gardening impact on the environment and human health. The work has ranged from desktop analyses of published research, own field and laboratory research, and supervising and supporting collaborative MSc, PhDs, and knowledge transfer partnership projects.

Our aim is to explore a range of issues that affect gardens and the environment, as well as the wildlife and the people who use these spaces. In effect, the scientific work looks at the "ecosystem services"—or benefits—that gardens and green spaces provide.

This book, for the first time, brings to life the science with practical ways of improving your garden. It is such an exciting time for all those who love plants and gardens. And this is just the start.

Professor Alistair Griffiths
Director of Science and Collections
Royal Horticultural Society

RHS Garden Wisley is the flagship garden of the Royal Horticultural Society, and home of the new National Center for Horticultural Science and Learning.

My plan for the Well-Being Garden at
RHS Garden Wisley is that it is made up
of a series of garden rooms, so that people
feel a sense of being enveloped by planting.
I want people to feel a sense of enclosure
and security, without blocking views.

Introduction

The health and well-being benefits of creating a calming, tranquil outdoor space have been amply proven, and for me, it's always a key consideration in the gardens that I design for clients, as well as in my own garden.

I like nothing more than to seek out the peace and greenery of my garden in order to relax and unwind, and having something to care for and nurture brings a sense of unpressured purpose, which is especially important for those with mental health issues. It's crucial to make your garden an inviting, beautiful space, one that is interesting, enraptures you, and invites your attention, that distracts you from mundane thoughts and encourages you to take time out to simply relax and enjoy.

Every garden has a boundary, and with a few simple tricks, this can be a comforting structure with a sense of enclosure and security that puts you at ease, rather than something that blocks everything out. Create a space that will capture your interest and encourage you to focus on something other than your daily stresses. A meandering path will discreetly slow your pace as you walk along it, perhaps toward a tranquil seating area or secluded garden room covered in plants, or a soothing water feature bubbling away, waiting to be discovered.

Fragrance can lift a mood or relax an anxious mind, and there are myriad plants that offer perfumes to calm or to excite. Experiment with them around seating areas, on pergolas or trellises, so that you get the full benefit of their scent. Plant them along pathways to encourage passers-by to brush past them, releasing their aromas and enhancing the sensual experience.

I'm a great believer in incorporating textures to distract the mind and encourage users to engage with and focus on the garden—soft, tactile shrubs such as rosemary that yearn to be touched, grasses that sway gently in the wind, or a blend of natural and human-made materials used through the hardscape.

Sounds are also important—to block out unwanted noise or to provide a soothing distraction. Water features are ideal for this, as well as providing an attractive focal point that bounces sunlight around dark corners.

Your garden is your space, and with a little thought and careful planning, you can transform it into a well-being haven that is your own personal retreat from everyday stresses.

Matt Keightley
Award-winning landscape designer

HOPE ON THE HORIZON GARDEN

This garden was designed as a serene, contemplative space for veterans recovering from the traumas of conflict. The planting flows from white to blues and purples, offset by *Stipa* grasses that catch the sunlight and blow gently in the breeze. Design by Matt Keightley.

The Protective Garden

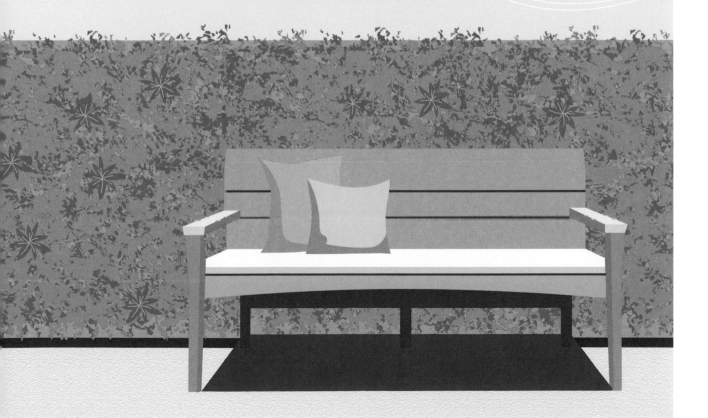

Introduction

Our gardens can help protect us, shielding us from air pollution and allergens, and filtering or masking intrusive noise.

Plants are constantly hard at work shielding us from noise and pollution and helping to improve our environment. Trees and shrubs, for instance, can trap harmful particles in the air caused by vehicle emissions, and research shows that greening up any surface—a wall, roof, or fence—will help reduce the levels of particulates in your garden. You can use plants to protect against noise pollution, too, while natural sounds, such as rustling plants or a tinkling water feature, can mask traffic and other sounds outside your garden. As well as shielding you from particulates and noise, plants can help to minimize the pollen and allergen presence in your garden, allowing you to enjoy your outside space all year round, even if you suffer from hay fever. It is also important to protect the wildlife in your garden by avoiding the use of pesticides and chemicals, and adopting a wildlife-friendly, integrated approach to pest control that will be healthier for you, your garden, and the environment.

Plants as potential pollution-busters

Vegetation can capture harmful pollutant particles and help to direct them away from people.

Many of us are regularly exposed to airborne pollutants such as emissions from industrial processes, gasoline and diesel engines, and other burning of fossil fuels. Research shows that plants can capture those pollutant particles, known as particulates, on their leaves, taking them out of circulation and improving local air quality. You can harness this for your own outdoor space, using trees, hedging, and shrubs to create a barrier against pollutants. If space is at a premium, climbers, trailing plants, and living walls or roofs offer alternative options.

HOW DO LEAVES TRAP PARTICLES?

All leaves trap small amounts of air pollutants, but some plants outperform others. Studies have found that those with hairy, scaly, waxy, and rough leaves are particularly effective (see opposite). Recent research showed that a yew canopy, for example, can accumulate four times more fine airborne particles than photinia, which has smoother leaves and is less dense. Likewise, the larger surface areas of complex leaf shapes are more effective than simpler ones. The amount each plant can trap depends on the concentration of pollutants in the air, humidity, wind speed and direction, and temperature.

Why it matters

According to the World Health Organization, 90 percent of the world's population breathe polluted air. Air pollution is linked to rising levels of respiratory diseases, cancer, stroke, heart disease, diabetes, obesity, dementia, and early death. Tiny, ultrafine particles of air pollution are the most dangerous, penetrating lung tissue to enter the bloodstream and even the placentas of pregnant women.

HAIRY LEAVES

Hairy leaves provide a larger surface area than smooth leaves and can capture particles on both sides. Particles (shown in red in the electron-microscope image above) are trapped in the spaces between the hairs. This stops particles being blown off and recirculated. Examples include cotoneaster (*Cotoneaster franchetii* and *C. coriaceus*) and flowering currant (*Ribes*).

COTONEASTER
(*Cotoneaster franchetii*)

SCALY LEAVES

Plants with scalelike, short, overlapping leaves provide a rough surface that increases air turbulence around the plant and allows for greater deposits of particles. Particles are trapped in the scales and also in the waxy coating of the cuticle layer (the outer surface of the leaf). Examples include red cedar (*Thuja plicata*) and lemon cypress (*Cupressus macrocarpa* 'Goldcrest').

RED CEDAR
(*Thuja plicata*)

WAXY LEAVES

Particulates are trapped and embedded in the waxy cuticle layer that surrounds the leaves. Examples include yew (*Taxus baccata*), holly (*Ilex aquifolium*), and laurustinus (*Viburnum tinus*).

YEW (*Taxus baccata*)

ROUGH LEAVES

Leaves with rough surfaces have uneven profiles that increase air turbulence around the plant, causing particles to attach to the ridges and grooves on the leaf's surface. Examples include hawthorn (*Crataegus monogyna*), hornbeam (*Carpinus betulus*), and Japanese rose (*Rosa rugosa*).

HAWTHORN
(*Crataegus monogyna*)

WHICH GREENERY IS BEST?

Trees planted in wide belts next to busy roads can be very effective at trapping toxic particles, with some high-performing tree species removing up to 20 times more particles than others. In Beijing, research showed that trees in the city center locked away 851 tons (772 tonnes) of particulate matter in a single year.

In broad, tree-lined streets, tree canopies tend to create air turbulence beneath them and allow for pollutant particles to be deposited onto leaf surfaces. The remaining particles disperse upward on the air currents. But in "street canyon" scenarios, avenues of large trees can worsen air pollution's effects.

The "street canyon" effect

An avenue of large trees in a "street canyon," where tall buildings line both sides of a narrow road, can worsen pollution at street level. This is

A hedge can form a protective barrier between your garden and a source of emissions, and then funnel particles upward to be dispersed.

because large tree canopies prevent pollutants emitted by traffic from dispersing into the air higher up (small trees may not have this effect).

In these settings, hedges can outperform trees (see opposite). Hedges form a barrier that traps particles while allowing dispersal of toxic fumes. Research in 2018 found that roadside hedges could cut black carbon (a sooty black material in emissions) by up to 63 percent, while roadside trees alone had no effect on reducing pollution at breathing height.

Why plants outperform fences

Compared to a fence panel, hedges, with their multiple leaf surfaces and greater depth, offer a much larger area on which to trap particles. The leaf-area index system demonstrates this: it calculates how many square metres a plant would cover if the leaves from a 1sq m (11sq ft) area of the plant were laid side by side on the ground (see right). Some species trap particulates on both sides of their leaves, increasing the quantity they filter from the air.

11sq ft (1sq m) area of privet shrub

When laid out on the ground, the leaves cover an area of about 33sq ft (3sq m)

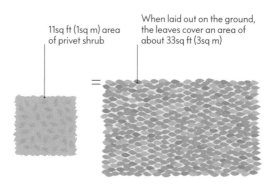

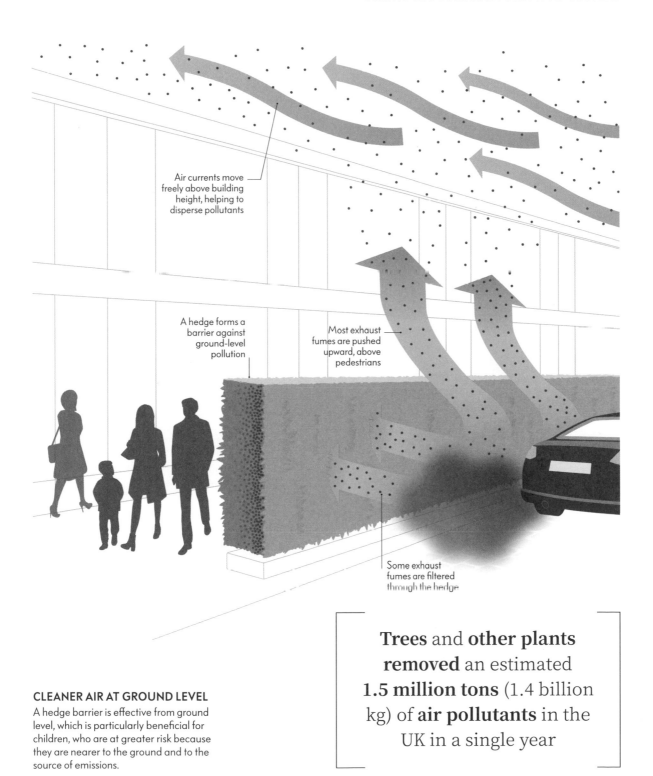

Air currents move freely above building height, helping to disperse pollutants

A hedge forms a barrier against ground-level pollution

Most exhaust fumes are pushed upward, above pedestrians

Some exhaust fumes are filtered through the hedge

Trees and **other plants removed** an estimated **1.5 million tons** (1.4 billion kg) of **air pollutants** in the UK in a single year

CLEANER AIR AT GROUND LEVEL

A hedge barrier is effective from ground level, which is particularly beneficial for children, who are at greater risk because they are nearer to the ground and to the source of emissions.

MAXIMIZE YOUR HEDGE'S EFFECTIVENESS

Healthy hedges with plenty of leaf cover will usually be better than a fence at trapping pollution. Some leaf types are more effective than others (see p.21), so your choice of plant will have an impact on your hedge's efficiency as a pollution barrier. The condition of your hedge, its height, width, and density are also important factors (see below).

Good maintenance

Pruning helps to keep hedges dense, which is important for creating the maximum surface area onto which pollutant particles can attach. It will also help to keep the hedge's shape compact and bushy at the base.

If you want a formal hedge, you'll need to trim it two or three times in the growing season. For informal hedges, an annual trim should be enough. The timing depends on the plant type, but all hedges benefit from pruning right after planting to encourage them to grow out as well as up. A well-grown hedge will support wildlife, so avoid pruning between March and August to avoid disturbing nesting birds.

Choosing your hedge

Look for plants that naturally make dense barriers, as they create a network of branches for capturing particles. The six examples shown opposite all performed well in scientific studies examining their pollution-fighting potential. If these plant types aren't suitable for your space and growing conditions, look for ones with similar characteristics, such as leaf type (see p.21). Although deciduous shrubs and trees lose their leaves annually, some, such as hornbeam, can hold their leaves until late winter. Evergreen hedges, such as cotoneaster and holly, keep their coverage year round. Use the checklist (see p.27) to help you choose.

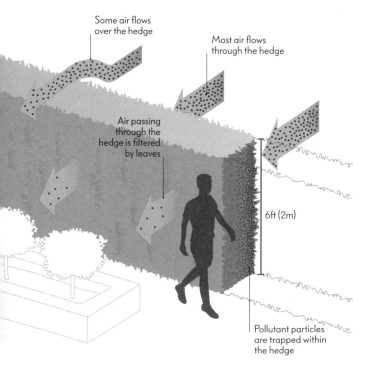

Some air flows over the hedge

Most air flows through the hedge

Air passing through the hedge is filtered by leaves

6ft (2m)

Pollutant particles are trapped within the hedge

SCIENCE IN ACTION

Dense hedges that allow air to flow through them capture more particles than gappy hedges or hedges that block airflow. The most effective for filtering pollutants are permeable hedges between 3ft (1m) and 6ft (2m) high.

1

4

5

2

6

GOOD PERFORMERS

Research is still ongoing into which plants are best at capturing pollutants, but these plants are so far among the best performers.

DECIDUOUS

1 Hawthorn (*Crataegus monogyna*) has dark red berries in fall.

2 Hornbeam (*Carpinus betulus*) has yellow foliage in fall.

3 Japanese barberry (*Berberis thunbergii*) has red and orange foliage in fall.

Other options
Flowering currant (*Ribes*), bird cherry (*Prunus padus*), dogwood (*Cornus*)

EVERGREEN

4 Cotoneaster (*Cotoneaster franchetti*) has orange-red fruit in fall.

5 English yew (*Taxus baccata*) needs clipping only once a year.

6 Holly (*Ilex aquifolium*) has bright red berries on female plants in fall.

Other options
Boxwood (*Buxus sempervirens*), laurustinus (*Viburnum tinus*), spindle (*Euonymus japonicus*), western red cedar (*Thuja plicata*), firethorn (*Pyracantha*)

3

Planting a double hedge

Plant shrubs in two rows to help create a dense hedge base. Line up the plants in the second row to offset the gaps in the first row. The planting distance depends on the size of the plants and what species you choose. Beech, for example, needs about 2ft (60cm) between plants, as shown below.

2ft (60cm)

2ft (60cm)

DESIGNING YOUR POLLUTION BARRIER

Your garden may be big enough for a solid shield of pollutant-filtering trees and hedging all around the perimeter, or you might have a smaller area to play with. No matter what size your garden is, you can use planting to create effective barriers against pollution.

Green barriers

Your choice of planting for any barrier hedge will of course depend on factors such as climate, soil, and available space (see checklist opposite).

If you live in a high-pollution area, you may want to choose evergreen planting, so that your barrier is effective all year round. Although fences alone aren't as effective in trapping pollution as hedges, you could install some fencing until your hedge establishes. Mature trees and shrubs will give your hedge a head start, but this impacts on cost. If space simply doesn't allow for hedging, encourage wall shrubs or climbers to cover walls and fences, as they can still help trap pollution: a study of ivy screens grown alongside a busy main road in the UK showed that 11sq ft (1sq m) of ivy screen is likely to remove 145 million particulates a day.

Hedges as features

One way to turn your hedge into a feature is to alternate materials, interspersing hedging with paneling, such as wood or a feature wall. Gabion walls—metal cages filled with stone or wood—create visual interest while also being havens for wildlife. However, introducing these hard materials will reduce your hedge's potential to capture pollution.

Another option is to alternate your planting, interspersing different leaf types and colors. For example, you could combine green and copper beech, or green with purple berberis.

Many hedging plants are also attractive as stand-alone plants, so if space is at a premium, you could simply plant single shrubs—a cloud-pruned box, for example, or a Japanese spiraea. A stand-alone shrub can still help filter pollution, and your one plant can offer added interest, such as blossoms and berries, while providing food and habitat for local wildlife, too.

Hedges as partitions

If you have space, you can use hedges to break up an area, creating "rooms" in your garden—and adding filtering screens. Even if space is limited, don't discount the idea of a short hedge. It can help to define your space and create a subtle extra pollution shield.

A row of pleached trees forming a hedge next to a boundary will capture more pollution than the wall alone could.

Checklist

Ask yourself these questions when designing and choosing your hedging:

- Do you want it to act as a background or to be a statement feature?
- Do you want it to be evergreen or deciduous?
- Does it need to be fast- or slow-growing? Will it be pregrown or will you grow it *in situ*?
- What conditions do you have? Does the hedge need to be best suited to full sun, partial sun, or shade?
- How hardy will it need to be?
- Will it need to be drought-resistant or able to survive in wet climates?
- Do you want a single plant type or mixed planting?

Using colors other than green offers variety, or you could mix colors (as here) for different effects.

Soften hard edges and create a pollution-trapping barrier by growing a climber on walls.

One medium-sized shrub can capture **30 diesel cars'** worth of **pollution each year**

27

NO ROOM
FOR A HEDGE?

Even if you have only a small outside space, you can still harness the power of plants to fight pollution by planting every available surface—any plant barrier will help to clean the air around your home. Trail plants off your balcony, train climbers up fences and walls, create a green roof on your shed, or even build a living wall. At the same time, houseplants can boost air quality inside your home.

Living walls in their many forms—from simple climbers to more structured versions—are an effective way to trap pollution and provide food and shelter for wildlife.

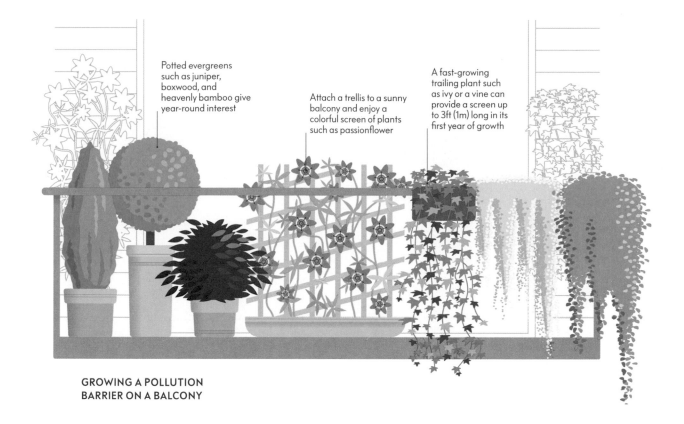

Potted evergreens such as juniper, boxwood, and heavenly bamboo give year-round interest

Attach a trellis to a sunny balcony and enjoy a colorful screen of plants such as passionflower

A fast-growing trailing plant such as ivy or a vine can provide a screen up to 3ft (1m) long in its first year of growth

GROWING A POLLUTION BARRIER ON A BALCONY

No flower beds, no problem

If you have a balcony, plants will not only make it more attractive, they can also help screen pollution. Focus on evergreens for year-round foliage. You could have a mix of shrubs, such as boxwood or bamboo, for variety and interest; trailing plants will drape delicate curtains of greenery. Ivy is versatile as a climber or trailing plant, with variegated varieties giving contrast.

Climbers can provide large surface areas for trapping particulates, so use containers to plant climbers or shrubs up against a house wall or fence. Choose plant types that will thrive in a container and suit your climate, and remember to feed them regularly. Try flower-bearing plants such as passionflower or potato vine for added interest, but be sure to water frequently if they are planted in a rain shadow. Even on a wall that is north- or east-facing, or shaded, there are plants that will thrive, such as roses, star jasmine, climbing hydrangea, and spindle.

Living walls and green roofs

Installing a living wall can be a worthwhile investment. It will need frequent watering, so most are designed with drip-irrigation systems. Pots that hook onto railings or fabric living wall planters are cheaper options. You can also green up the roofs of sheds, bike shelters, or storage bins. Plant a mix of shallow-rooted, drought-tolerant grasses and creeping plants here, or lay ready-planted sedum matting.

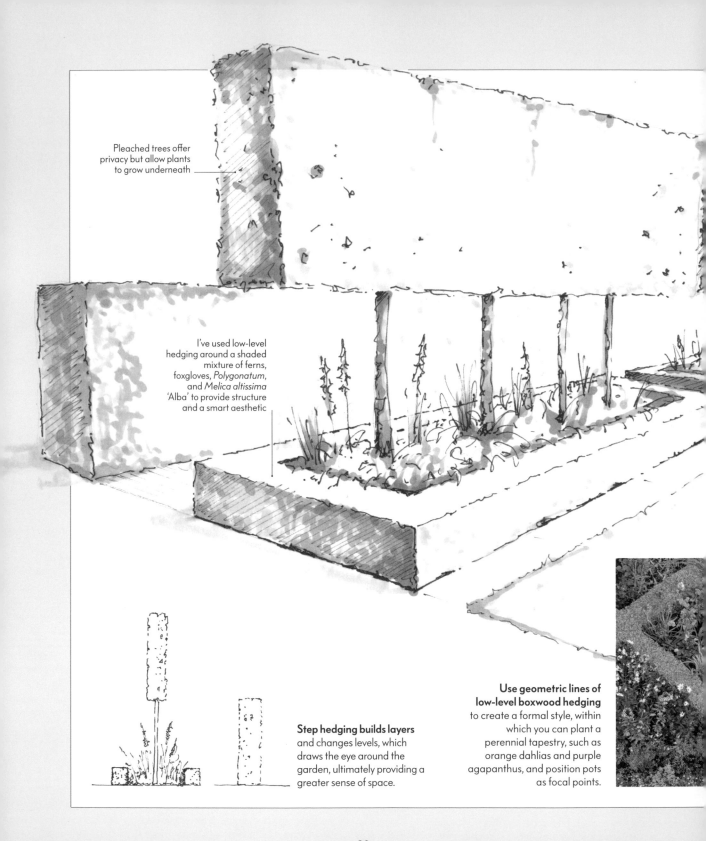

Pleached trees offer privacy but allow plants to grow underneath

I've used low-level hedging around a shaded mixture of ferns, foxgloves, *Polygonatum*, and *Melica altissima* 'Alba' to provide structure and a smart aesthetic

Step hedging builds layers and changes levels, which draws the eye around the garden, ultimately providing a greater sense of space.

Use geometric lines of low-level boxwood hedging to create a formal style, within which you can plant a perennial tapestry, such as orange dahlias and purple agapanthus, and position pots as focal points.

Designing your boundary

Enclosure is an important part of a well-being garden. A space divided into separate rooms, or areas flanked and enveloped by hedging, can make someone feel safe, secure, and comforted.

Something as simple as a hedge can be incredibly versatile as a boundary, no matter what size, shape, or style your garden. The geometry of low hedging, the intricacy of patterned parterres, or the anchoring structure of individual shapes can add a whole new dimension to a garden. Hedging can also be an outdoor art to enhance any design style; topiary is the perfect complement to classic Georgian architecture or the contained symmetry of a Victorian city terrace.

Hedging adds layers and depth, too, drawing the eye through a space or stopping you in your tracks by framing another part of the garden. When choosing your hedging plant, consider what it will look like through the year—you don't have to stick to evergreens, as some deciduous plants will retain a strong skeletal presence in winter.

Pleached trees are a great solution for adding height and screening in an overlooked garden, particularly in urban areas. Both evergreen and deciduous trees, such as the hornbeam above, will work.

Plants as potential soundproofing

Noise can be an irritation that undermines your well-being, but with some clever design tricks, you can restore quiet.

Noise pollution is not just annoying, it's also bad for our physical and mental health, and it negatively affects wildlife. While completely soundproofing your garden is unrealistic, you can reduce the intensity of surrounding noise through effective design and planting. Layering different types of vegetation can block sound at multiple heights, and introducing natural sounds—such as rustling leaves or running water—will help to distract the ear and mask the hum of traffic or noise from neighboring gardens.

DESIGNING FOR QUIET

According to the World Health Organization, noise is second only to airborne fine particles (see p.20) in polluting health. It's linked to a range of issues, from tinnitus and hearing loss to elevated blood pressure, sleep disturbance, and mental health problems. But it also impacts animals, who rely on sounds for various behaviors such as attracting a mate, locating food, or detecting predators.

While hard surfaces reflect sound, plants can help diffuse noise pollution, as can some landscaping features, such as lawns. Sounds interact with plants or structures through reflection, absorption, scattering, and diffraction (see opposite). Trees with smooth trunks, for example, redirect sounds by bouncing or bending them around the garden. Textured surfaces, such as rough-barked branches, twigs, and leaves, scatter sound in many directions, lessening its effects in any one place. Soft, spongy surfaces, such as grass, fleshy leaves, and some more porous barks make effective sound absorbers. If you yearn for a pocket of tranquillity, layer plants of different heights and textures to create boundaries for quiet zones.

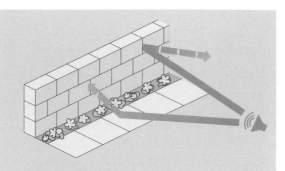

REFLECTION

When sound hits a solid surface (such as a wall or a paved driveway), it is not absorbed. Instead, the sound waves reflect off the solid surface at the same angle as they hit them but travel in a different direction. Surfaces such as concrete reflect almost all the sound waves that travel across them, which makes paved front gardens a noisy option.

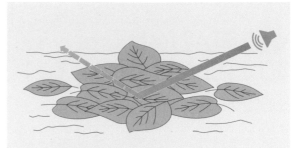

ABSORPTION

When sound waves encounter soft, porous surfaces, they are partly absorbed, reflecting noise more faintly. Soft, porous surfaces, such as grass, soil, and leaf litter, and plant parts, such as stems, leaves, and branches, can all absorb sound. Rough bark and thick, fleshy leaves absorb sound well due to their large surface areas and sometimes spongy textures, and this absorption dampens noise pollution.

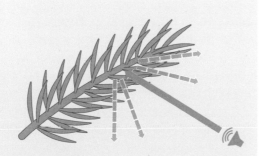

SCATTERING

When sound hits a surface with faces that are at many angles to the sound wave (a conifer twig, for instance), much of the wave is scattered in multiple directions, reducing its impact. Although more solid uneven surfaces such as gravel also scatter sound waves, leaves—being less rigid—are better at reducing sound because they vibrate and have a greater scattering effect.

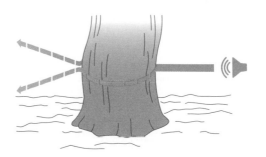

DIFFRACTION

Diffraction helps sound waves to "bend" around obstacles in their path, such as a tree trunk, but also to spread out once they have passed through small openings, such as gaps between plants or in hedges.

LAYER VEGETATION TO FILTER SOUND

Including a variety of levels of vegetation in the garden not only creates structure and interest, but can also help to filter sound. A combination of trees, shrubs, and groundcover, all at different heights, with an area of soft, porous ground in front, offers an ideal natural sound barrier. In smaller spaces, a mixture of shrubs and low-growing plants can muffle traffic noise.

As a simple rule, try to create a barrier of plants that you can't see through. Remember that plants in your neighbors' gardens may form part of an effective barrier for you, too. Sound coming from the prevalent wind direction appears amplified, and a row of trees—yours or your neighbors'—can reduce sound levels.

Rows of **trees** and **hedges** can reduce noise by **6** to **9 decibels**

Block sound at ground level

Trees and shrubs can reduce high-pitched sounds such as sirens and some deeper sounds such as motorbikes. Trees with low-growing branches make excellent sound barriers to noise generated at or near ground level, such as vehicle engines. Trees lacking lower branches allow some of this noise to pass through, but bushy shrubs or hedges planted around their bases can help to absorb and scatter ground-level noise.

Mix up leaf shapes

Leaves absorb some sound energy by vibrating, then reflect and diffract the rest. Generally, trees and shrubs with larger, thicker leaves and a greater leaf-area index (see p.22) perform best as a sound barrier, but plant types vary in effectiveness. A study of six evergreen trees and shrubs found that ovate (egg-shaped) leaves perform better than long, narrow leaves, but when it came to blocking out low-frequency sounds, the narrow-leaved deodar cedar was best. By using a mix of shrubs and trees with varying leaf shapes and densities, you'll create the best noise buffer across different frequencies.

Understanding sound

Sound is a traveling wave of compressed and expanded air. Sounds at high frequencies, such as a soprano singing a high C note, has a wavelength of about 1ft (34cm). The low rumble of traffic has a wavelength of about 11ft (3.4m). To be effective at reducing sound, barriers need to be taller than the wavelength along the direction of travel. So low-lying foliage and small shrubs can reduce high frequencies, while trees are effective at blocking midrange frequencies.

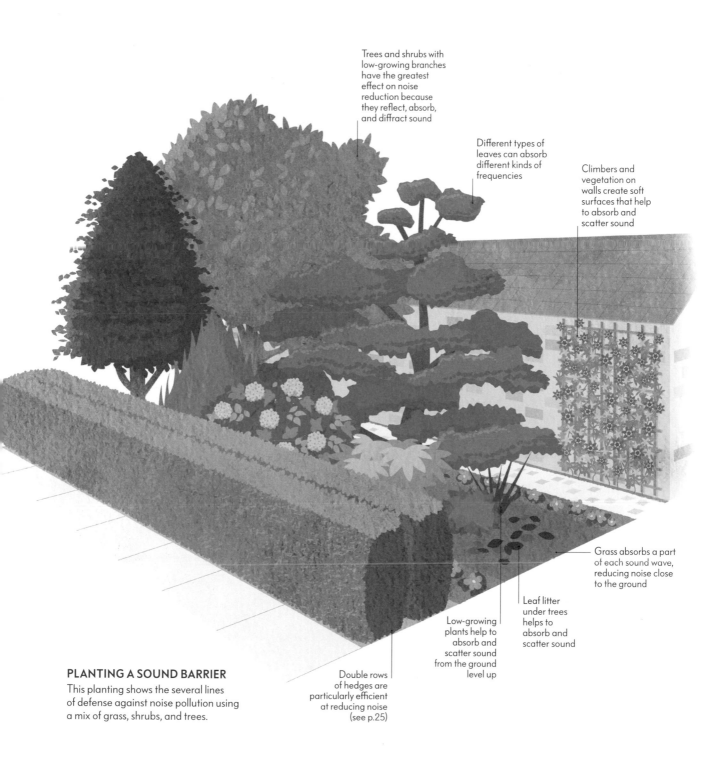

Trees and shrubs with low-growing branches have the greatest effect on noise reduction because they reflect, absorb, and diffract sound

Different types of leaves can absorb different kinds of frequencies

Climbers and vegetation on walls create soft surfaces that help to absorb and scatter sound

Grass absorbs a part of each sound wave, reducing noise close to the ground

Leaf litter under trees helps to absorb and scatter sound

Low-growing plants help to absorb and scatter sound from the ground level up

Double rows of hedges are particularly efficient at reducing noise (see p.25)

PLANTING A SOUND BARRIER

This planting shows the several lines of defense against noise pollution using a mix of grass, shrubs, and trees.

PLANTING FOR NOISE-BUFFERING

If you have room for a tree in your garden, it will make a good sound barrier, and trees with a good-sized trunk and network of branches, and a dense canopy, are more effective. If you don't have the space, or are concerned about root damage to buildings, trees and shrubs in containers are a good solution. Containers give plants additional height and, depending on materials, can also absorb sound. A hedge or a group of shrubs can also form an effective sound barrier.

Laurels, with their thick foliage, are good candidates for a large shrub or a hedge and, being evergreen, give protection against noise all year round. Dense trees with ovate leaves, such as beech, and some conifers, such as cedar, are good options (see opposite).

Dense and layered

At ground level, soil helps to absorb noise, and earth banks have been shown to make good sound barriers. Try landscaping your garden with varying levels to create quiet zones. Layer your planting vertically, small to large plants, to help trap sound from sources at different heights. Situate your plants as near to the source of the noise as possible, where they will have the most impact, and plant them as close together as you can, allowing for growth.

Climbers with thick foliage can absorb noise above head height, and modular living walls are good at absorbing low-frequency sounds (see p.170).

Even if you don't have a garden, an array of plants in containers can act as a sound barrier, while climbers help to absorb sounds reflecting off walls.

In a small space, plant your barrier along the boundary of your garden, as close to the noise source as possible.

Rosemary, agapanthus, and other plants provide a variety of leaf shapes and plant heights that will absorb a range of different sound frequencies.

PLANTS FOR SOUNDPROOFING

Plants with dense, heavy leaves with an ovate or elliptical shape are good sound-absorbers. Some conifers perform well too.

EVERGREEN

- **Photinia** (*Photinia serrulata*) is effective at absorbing high-frequency sounds.
- **Deodar cedar** (*Cedrus deodara*) is a conifer that is particularly good at absorbing low frequencies.
- **Portugal laurel** (*Prunus lusitanica*) is a shrub or tree with a spreading habit and ovate leaves.
- **Holly** (*Ilex* species and cultivars) has a dense habit with lots of branches and large leaves.
- **Italian cypress** (*Cupressus sempervirens*) is a conifer with dense foliage that is good for absorbing sound.

Other options with dense foliage
English yew (*Taxus baccata*); *Thuja*; *Eucalyptus*; evergreen oak (*Quercus ilex*).

DECIDUOUS

- **Beech** (*Fagus sylvatica*) has ovate leaves, a shape shown to be effective at limiting noise.
- **Hornbeam** (*Carpinus betulus*) is a hardy, broad-leaved tree that keeps its leaves into winter.

NATURAL SOUNDS TO DISTRACT ATTENTION

Some noises, such as the background hum of traffic or the whirr of a nearby air-conditioning unit, are annoying rather than intrusively loud. Studies show that natural sounds such as birdsong; the rustling of windblown leaves, stems, or branches; or the tinkling of falling or flowing water can mask noise or distract our attention from it. A Swedish study showed that people recovered from stress more quickly when listening to natural sounds, such as moving water and birdsong, than they did listening to city noises. Another Swedish study showed that participants most valued urban green spaces when they could hear a variety of different birdsong, which studies show has a soothing effect on most of us (see p.116).

Water sounds

Road traffic noise is mostly made up of mid- to low frequencies. Although large flows of water pouring into hollow spaces make the kind of low-frequency sound that can cover traffic noise, studies show that we rate these sounds poorly. Instead, we prefer listening to higher-frequency, variable water sounds. While we can't entirely mask traffic noises with higher-frequency water sounds, we still find them pleasantly distracting.

You don't have to have space for a large fountain to distract you from unwanted noise: intermittent splashes for a more soothing murmur can be just as effective. While big ponds or rills that run the length of your garden look dramatic (see p.113), you can include water features in your design in other ways. In smaller spaces, incorporate mini waterfalls mounted on boundary or house walls to provide a tinkling sound. Install a pump in small ponds or containers for a continuous cascade. Note that studies show that we prefer the sound of water falling onto water, rather than on hard surfaces.

Water bubbling over pebbles, or steel or stone balls, or continually pouring out of a container, will create soothing, diverting sounds. Pair these with rustling grasses and whispering leaves for your own peaceful paradise (see pp.40–41).

Rills provide a continuous relaxing sound, spilling into a pond below (left). In smaller spaces, they can be mounted onto low or boundary walls.

Water trickling down a transparent wall recreates the rhythmic, relaxing sound of rain falling on a window (above).

Pumps installed inside water containers will create small bubbling cascades that have a calming, distracting sound (above).

Small gardens can welcome the soothing sound of moving water with a simple pot and a trickling cascade (left).

Plants that rustle and whisper

Along with other planting strategies, the gentle whispering sounds made by wind blowing through trees can help to divert our attention from or mask noise pollution. In addition to conifers, there are many other kinds of trees and shrubs that catch the lightest breezes and tremble or rustle hypnotically, making sounds that distract the ear from unwanted noise.

The type of sound a plant makes depends on the speed of the wind, as well as the size, shape, weight, and stiffness of the leaves, the stiffness and size of the stem and stalks, and the distance between branches or leaves.

Grass types with flexible stems will rustle as they bend, giving a soft undercurrent of sound in a gentle breeze. Try large clumps of bamboo and grasses such as *Stipa* and *Miscanthus* (see opposite). The dried fall leaves of deciduous hedging plants also make rustling sounds that can distract. The needles of conifers, and the small, light leaves of trees such as birch and aspen, create high-pitched, whispering sounds.

Rattling and clapping sounds

In late summer and fall, plants that have seedheads can create occasional gentle rattling sounds as the stems move and sway in the wind, shaking the dried seeds inside. Or, for year-round distraction, try species with architectural, strap-shaped leaves or large, stiff leaves that make louder, more percussive sounds as they slap together in the wind.

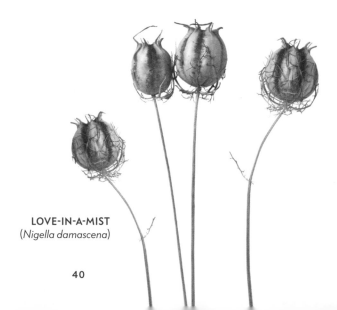

LOVE-IN-A-MIST
(*Nigella damascena*)

PLANTS TO HELP MASK NOISE

1 Chilean bamboo (*Chusquea culeou*) The lance-shaped leaves of this clump-forming, noninvasive bamboo make gentle rustling sounds in the breeze.

2 Giant feather grass (*Stipa gigantea*) This tufted evergreen grass has arching linear leaves that rustle in the wind.

3 Birch (*Betula pendula*) The delicate foliage of birch makes distracting whispering sounds.

4 Turkish sage (*Phlomis russeliana*) The seedpods of this perennial create soft rattling sounds in the breeze.

5 Cabbage palm (*Cordyline australis*) The long, sword-shaped leaves of this small evergreen tree can make clapping sounds in the wind.

Other options
Rustling plants: sinuate bamboo (*Phyllostachys flexuosa*), beech (*Fagus sylvatica*), winter leaves of hornbeam hedge (*Carpinus betulus*), maiden grass (*Miscanthus sinensis*)
Whispering leaves: silver linden (*Tilia tomentosa*), aspen (*Populus tremula*), golden weeping willow (*Salix* x *sepulcralis* var. *chrysocoma*), black pine (*Pinus nigra*)
Rattling seeds: bladder senna (*Colutea arborescens*), asphodel (*Asphodeline lutea*), love-in-a-mist (*Nigella damascena*)
Clapping leaves: New Zealand flax (*Phormium tenax*), windmill palm (*Trachycarpus fortunei*)

I chose mullein and globe thistle for their delicate seedheads, which prolong their season of interest from their summer flowers through to winter

Scots pine makes a soothing sound as it rustles in the wind

If you're looking for a small tree to rustle in the wind, try a dwarf mountain pine tree for the unique, rhythmic clicking sound the stiff needles make.

Designing around sound

Drifts of Mexican feather grass grow among stands of white agapanthus and *Nepeta racemosa* 'Six Hills Giant'.

Gardens naturally stimulate the senses, and the use of sound in a space can be wonderfully hypnotic and soothing, helping your brain to reboot and your body to relax. Position trees or grasses in more exposed parts of the garden so that their movement in the breeze creates calming, rustling, or whispering sounds. Use grasses in large blocks or drifts to exaggerate their gentle movement, and to add height and depth to a planting design. Grasses are the perfect partner to the seedheads of perennials, which appear in late summer and can make quiet rattling sounds as they move.

Plants need not be the only source of sound in the garden. Install a bird table or a feeder to encourage birds into your green space and benefit from the soothing qualities of their singing, or add a trickling water feature to enjoy its calming effect.

Ornamental grasses, such as feather top and tufted hair grass, exaggerate the movement in the bed as they sway in the breeze. Planted among flowering perennials, they add height and depth to a scheme

Seedheads on perennials, such as these alliums, add to the soundscape of your garden as they quietly rattle in the wind, while the delicate structures dusted with frost create visual interest in winter.

Creating a low-allergen garden

With the right plants, your garden can be a haven—even for allergy-sufferers—all year round.

Although it's not possible to eliminate all pollen-producing plants from a garden—or even desirable, since they are beneficial to bees and other pollinating insects—some plants will actually remove pollen from the air by trapping the grains. Other plants produce much lower levels of pollen, and so, with careful design and planting, allergy-sufferers can enjoy their gardens throughout the year.

POLLEN AND ALLERGIES

As any hay fever sufferer knows, not all plants bring a sense of well-being. For the estimated 10 to 30 percent of adults and 40 percent of children globally who suffer from hay fever, being outside when the pollen count is high is not always an idyllic prospect.

Pollen is produced by the male reproductive parts of a plant and transferred, either by wind, water, or via insects and animals, to the stigma, the female part of a plant, for pollination. Fertilization then takes place and the plant produces seeds.

Sex matters

Perfect-flowered plants, such as some foxgloves, lilies, and roses, have both male and female parts together in the same flower. Monoecious plants, such as birch and hazel, have separate male and female flowers on the same plant, while dioecious plants, such as holly, juniper, and some grasses, have male plants with only male flowers and female plants with only female flowers. Male dioecious plants produce pollen, and the female plants produce fruits or seeds but no pollen.

Some plants produce much less pollen than others (see opposite), and sterile plants, which have no male or female flowers, produce no pollen at all. Sterile plants, low-pollen producers, and the females of dioecious plants are the best choices for a low-allergen garden.

44

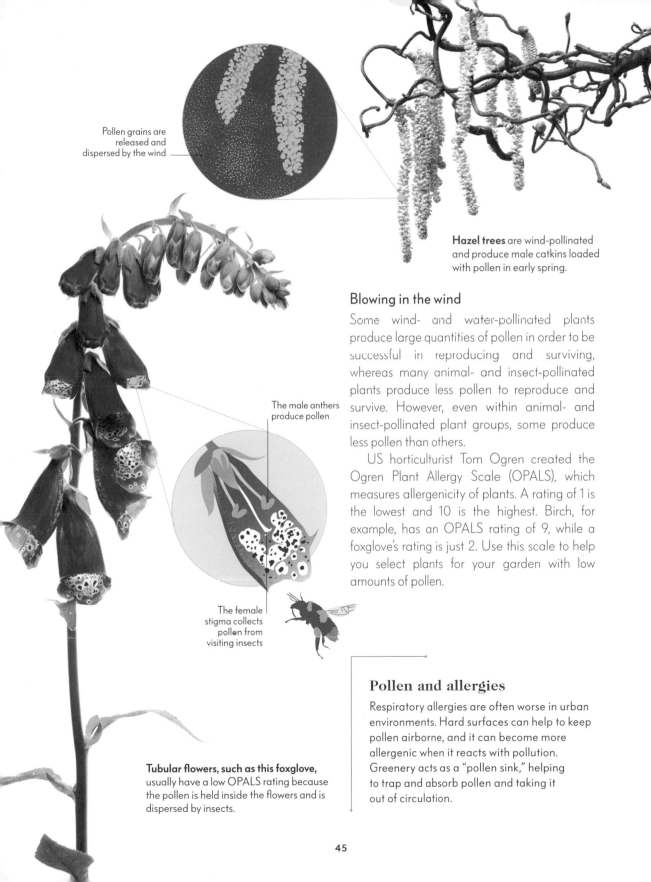

Pollen grains are released and dispersed by the wind

Hazel trees are wind-pollinated and produce male catkins loaded with pollen in early spring.

The male anthers produce pollen

The female stigma collects pollen from visiting insects

Tubular flowers, such as this foxglove, usually have a low OPALS rating because the pollen is held inside the flowers and is dispersed by insects.

Blowing in the wind

Some wind- and water-pollinated plants produce large quantities of pollen in order to be successful in reproducing and surviving, whereas many animal- and insect-pollinated plants produce less pollen to reproduce and survive. However, even within animal- and insect-pollinated plant groups, some produce less pollen than others.

US horticulturist Tom Ogren created the Ogren Plant Allergy Scale (OPALS), which measures allergenicity of plants. A rating of 1 is the lowest and 10 is the highest. Birch, for example, has an OPALS rating of 9, while a foxglove's rating is just 2. Use this scale to help you select plants for your garden with low amounts of pollen.

Pollen and allergies

Respiratory allergies are often worse in urban environments. Hard surfaces can help to keep pollen airborne, and it can become more allergenic when it reacts with pollution. Greenery acts as a "pollen sink," helping to trap and absorb pollen and taking it out of circulation.

DESIGNING A HAVEN FOR ALLERGY SUFFERERS

Allergies don't have to prevent you enjoying your garden. With a few clever strategies, you can design a space that will minimize pollen levels and ease allergy symptoms.

Pick your flowers

Colorful, eye-catching flowers, such as peonies, violets, and pansies, produce very little airborne pollen and these, along with flowers that attract bees and other pollinating insects, such as penstemon and antirrhinum, are generally the best choices for hayfever sufferers. Most double flowers also produce very little pollen, and while they do not provide much food for pollinators, some, such as climbing roses, offer refuges and nesting sites for other wildlife.

Plants with hooded or tubular flowers, including foxgloves and agapanthus, have low OPALS ratings. Ornamental grasses, single-flowered daisies, and chrysanthemums, on the other hand, should be avoided. If you really love the look of ornamental grasses, try female grasses or strappy-leaved foliage plants such as *Libertia* or *Phormium,* which have insect-pollinated flowers and a lower OPALS rating.

Intensely scented plants such as wisteria and jasmine may trigger sensitivities to smell, so steer clear of these, too.

Lose the lawn

Lawns can be great for wildlife, but are not ideal for allergy sufferers, so consider other ground cover (see p.178) or opt for gravel or decking.

Hard surfaces can help to keep pollen airborne, so choose greenery to trap pollen grains from the air. Interlace paving with ground-cover plants, such as creeping thyme, that will trap pollen grains and soften hard edges. If you can't bear to lose your lawn, make sure that it is kept short to prevent the grass from flowering.

Choosing a hedge

It's impossible to banish all pollen from your garden, but you can make sure that it is easily blown away by installing permeable boundaries, such as trellises, to increase air flow. You could also try planting a low-allergen hedge along the windward side of your garden to capture pollen before it reaches you.

Opt for hedging plants that produce flowers, rather than catkins, and that have scaly or hairy leaves to trap pollen and pollutant particles (see p.21), such as hawthorn, *Choisya, Pittosporum,* and *Escallonia.* Female forms of dioecious plants, such as a berry-producing female holly plant, are also attractive and effective, but steer clear of privet, which has an OPALS rating of 9.

Your tree options

While many trees, including birch, hazel, and junipers, are wind-pollinated and best avoided, there are some beautiful flowering species, such as apple, cherry, and mountain ash, that produce very little airborne pollen and are perfect for small to medium-sized gardens.

LOW-ALLERGEN PLANTS

These plants all have a low OPALS rating, making them good choices for an allergy-friendly garden.

1 Snapdragon (*Antirrhinum*) has two-lipped flowers that come in a range of colors. OPALS rating: 1.

2 Female silver-margined holly (*Ilex aquifolium* 'Argentea Marginata') bears bright red berries in fall. OPALS rating: 1.

3 Whitebeam (*Sorbus aria*) is a deciduous tree that produces clusters of white flowers in spring and red berries in early fall. OPALS rating: 3.

4 Clematis (*Clematis armandii*) bears scented, star-shaped, creamy-white flowers in spring. OPALS rating: 3.

5 Garden pinks (*Dianthus*) have small sprays of fragrant, saucer-shaped flowers in a range of colors. OPALS rating: 3.

6 African lily (*Agapanthus*) bears spherical heads of trumpet-shaped blue, occasionally white, flowers in summer. OPALS rating: 2.

Wind-borne pollen can travel more than **1,000 miles (1,600km)** in **36 hours**, according to a **US** study

A LOW-ALLERGEN GARDEN
British designer Olivia Kirk's garden for the
University of Worcester uses swaths of
green and red foliage interspersed with
color from low-allergen flowers, including
irises, peonies, and astrantias.

Managing pests the natural way

Biodiversity offers a pesticide-free option for protecting your garden from pests without introducing toxins.

In the wild, the natural food chain keeps populations of plant-damaging pests in balance, and you can create the same conditions in your garden. Plant a wide variety of healthy plant types and species to support plenty of wildlife, choose disease-resistant varieties, and experiment with companion planting to protect from pests. At the same time, attract pest predators to your garden with a range of different strategies, such as installing a bug hotel or building a wildlife pond, or introduce natural organisms (called nematodes) that help fight pests.

AN INTEGRATED APPROACH

Prevention is better than cure, so making sure the plants you purchase are healthy—buying homegrown where possible—and maintaining them well will make them more resilient to pest damage. Good hygiene, such as regularly sterilizing garden tools, also reduces the spread of pests.

Until relatively recently, a common response to attacks by pests might have been to reach for pesticides. But these can harm other organisms as well as the target pests, including mycorrhizal fungi, which is so key to soil health (see pp.134–135). Metaldehyde, for example, a pesticide used to control slugs, has been shown to pose a threat to wildlife and pets. Pesticides can also leach into water sources. Some commercial

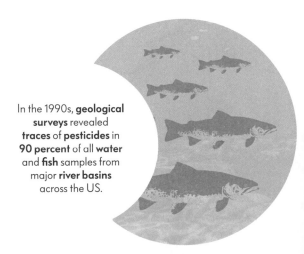

In the 1990s, **geological surveys** revealed **traces** of **pesticides** in **90 percent** of all **water** and **fish** samples from major **river basins** across the US.

In the US, **farmers and homeowners** apply about 500,000 tons (454,000 tonnes) of **pesticides** every year.

Invertebrates can detect **pheromones in nanogram** quantities—**1 nanogram** equals **0.000000001g**—which makes **pheromone traps** an effective way to monitor pests.

growers now employ an alternative, integrated approach, aiming to limit pests and plant damage to an acceptable level rather than eradicating them entirely. You can do this, too.

A variety of healthy plants

Aim for diversity in your garden—this will attract a range of wildlife and make plants less likely to succumb en masse to disease or attack by pests. Opt for disease-resistant types of vulnerable species if you're concerned about viral, fungal, or bacterial infection (see below right). Rotate vegetable crops each year to help prevent pest build-up in specific areas, as pests tend to reappear annually in the spots where their favorite species were last planted.

Monitor the number of pests in your garden by checking your plants regularly. Picking off pests from your plants before populations take hold may be all that's needed.

Bring in the predators

For many garden pests, there is a predator to prey on it (see pp.54–55). Create the optimum conditions for predators by providing suitable habitats and a water source (see pp.56–57). If you see a spike in a pest's population, find out if there are any of the pest's predators in your garden, as they may naturally reduce pest numbers. If pests persist, they are probably outnumbering your predators. In some cases, such as codling moth, you can then use

pheromone traps. Pheromones are chemicals that insects and other animals use to communicate with individuals of the same species. Pheromone traps attract specific pest species.

Controls as a last resort

If you have sustained periods of increased pest numbers and plant destruction, you may need to turn to organic products, which are made from natural ingredients, including soaps and oils, which smother pests. These are considered less damaging to the environment but can still harm beneficial organisms as well as pests, so use them as sparingly as possible.

Choose disease-resistant plants

Healthy plants well suited to their conditions will always cope with disease best, but you can buy many plants that are bred with resistance to certain diseases—ask for information at your garden center. For instance, a wide range of roses now have a genetic resistance to problems such as blackspot and powdery mildew, such as the English shrub rose 'The Lady Gardener'. Alternatively, choose plants that look similar and provide the same function in your planting scheme, but are not prone to a problem pest or disease. One example is Japanese holly, which is not afflicted by the blight that affects boxwood species.

PLANTS THAT PROTECT

There are two main strategies for using plants to protect other plants—companion planting and sacrificial planting. The former is the practice of growing two species of plants together to protect one of them from pest damage—the idea being that the protecting plant repels or draws pests away from the desired plant. Although there is little scientific evidence for the effectiveness of companion planting (apart from marigolds controlling root-knot nematodes), some gardeners swear by it. One reason it may work is that, by having more diversity in the garden, it's less likely that one invertebrate pest becomes a problem.

Plants are said to repel in different ways: insects dislike some pungent companion plants, such as alliums, because of their strong volatile oils. Other companion plants, such as marigolds, may make it harder for pests by masking their target plant's odors with their volatile oils, or by visually camouflaging the target plant.

Sacrificial planting uses two plantings that appeal to the same pest: one is the crop, and the other is the same, or similar, plant, which pests can reach more easily.

Other noninvasive pest controls include physical barriers such as netting around or over plants, keeping out pests such as carrot root fly. While mulching may protect plants against weeds, there is little evidence that mulch, egg shells, or horticultural grit will prevent pest damage. Recent research by the RHS, for example, found that physical barriers, such as pine bark mulch or copper tape, made no difference to slug and snail damage sustained by lettuce crops.

Sacrificial plants are grown in positions that are easier for pests to reach than the protected crop. Crops grown in pots or raised beds, for example, may be more difficult for slugs and snails to reach compared to crops grown in the ground.

GOOD COMPANIONS

These are some of the most commonly used companion plants that are also easy to grow:

1 Sunflowers (*Helianthus*) can create a barrier around crops, shielding them from pests.

2 Nasturtiums (*Tropaeolum majus*) are thought to be magnets for aphids—particularly blackfly, keeping them off your neighboring vegetable plants.

3 Marigolds (*Tagetes*) are commonly planted next to vegetables and are said to repel whitefly, root-knot nematodes, and carrot root fly, and attract pollinators with their scent.

4 Chives (*Allium schoenoprasum*) are often used as a companion plant to lure aphids away from ornamentals.

MAKING FRIENDS WITH PEST PREDATORS

The least invasive way to keep pest populations in check is to make the most of their natural predators. A wide range of predators visit our gardens, including birds, mammals (such as hedgehogs), and amphibians (frogs and toads). If you have space, installing a pond will prove to be a huge magnet for wildlife, particularly pest predators such as amphibians, which live near water (see pp.56–57).

Vast numbers of invertebrates—a huge group that includes insects, spiders, and worms—also come into our gardens, and they can prove to be invaluble pest predators too. Use the chart (see opposite) to find the predator to solve your insect pest problem, and create the habitats that will appeal to them. You can provide shelter for many of these predators with densely planted borders, bug hotels, compost, and log piles. You might also try to attract specific predators with their preferred food—for instance, open pollen-rich flowers provide nutrition for hoverflies, whose larvae eat aphids.

A single **ladybug** can eat **thousands** of **aphids** in its **lifetime**

Predators in the mail

Perhaps the quickest method of introducing pest predators to your garden is to buy them. You can get parasitic nematodes—microscopic, threadlike organisms that live in soil—in a garden center or order them online. Simply mix them with water and then water them into your soil. The nematodes seek out their host—such as a slug, vine weevil grub, leatherjacket, or ant—enter its body, and release bacteria that cause a fatal infection in the host. After killing the host, the nematodes reproduce inside its remains—now a soup of bacteria.
In the right conditions, these nematodes multiply but don't become a problem themselves since, once their prey's populations diminish, nematode numbers return to natural levels. You can also buy other pest predators, such as parasitoid wasps and predatory mites, to control aphids, whitefly, thrips, and other pests.

ATTRACT WILD PREDATORS FOR INSECT PESTS

Use this chart to find predators for some of the insect pests in your garden, and to help you create the habitats that will attract them.

IF YOU HAVE THIS PEST	YOU NEED THIS PREDATOR	SO CREATE THIS PREDATOR HABITAT
Vine weevil grubs Young slugs and snails	Centipedes	Compost pile Wood pile Bug hotel
Leatherjackets Vine weevils	Ground beetles	Compost pile Wood pile Bug hotel
Spider mites Scale insects Thrips White fly Aphids Mealybugs	Lacewings	Bug hotel Leaf litter
Aphids	Flying beetles	Bug hotel Foliage Leaf litter
Aphids	Flies and hoverflies	Pollen-rich plants

WELCOMING IN WILDLIFE

A wildlife pond is a wildlife magnet, which can help in the defense against pests. It will attract invertebrate predators as well as cater for the huge variety of other, larger predators that visit or live in gardens: birds (which need insects to feed themselves and their young), mammals (such as hedgehogs), amphibians (such as frogs and toads), and reptiles (such as slow worms).

Many of nature's pest-controllers, such as frogs, toads, newts, damselflies, and dragonflies, need water to breed in, and, with fewer wetlands and bodies of water in the countryside, a garden pond can help to support local populations. It can become a feeding ground for insect-eating birds and bats, and hedgehogs may visit to drink and eat slugs hiding among the waterside plants. There's no need to artificially introduce any animals to a new pond: wildlife will soon appear, with damselflies, dragonflies, pond skaters, and water boatmen likely to be the first visitors to arrive. Don't add fish to your pond—they'll eat other wildlife, particularly larvae.

All sizes fit the bill

Almost all shapes and sizes of ponds can be a home for wildlife, as long as the water is at least 8–12in (20–30cm) deep and kept oxygenated by one or two specific submerged plants (see opposite). Sink a watertight container into the ground or sit it on the ground. Alternatively, dig a pond-sized hole and use pond liner to make it watertight. Where possible, use rainwater to fill your pond—tap water is treated to make it safe to drink. With large ponds, a shallow "beach" area or ramp gives creatures safe access to the water. Water that is 2ft (60cm) deep or more in places will provide winter shelter for frogs, toads, and newts during icy spells.

Lay out your pond with everything it needs to support wildlife: oxygenating plants, stones, rocks, surrounding plants for hiding places, and a shallow edge for access.

A MAGNET FOR PREDATORS

A well-designed pond is one of the most effective pest-control elements in a garden, offering water and a habitat for an army of predators.

WHAT YOUR POND NEEDS

For your pond to attract a wide diversity of wildlife, you need:

1 Oxygenating plants, such as water crowfoot (*Ranunculus aquatilis*) and willow moss (*Fontinalis antipyretica*).

2 Surrounding plants, such as marsh marigold (*Caltha palustris*) and pickerel rush (*Pontederia cordata*), where creatures can hide.

3 Floating plants such as waterweed (*Elodea canadensis*) and, for large ponds only, white waterlily (*Nymphaea alba*), where creatures can perch.

4 Stones and rocks and a rotting branch or log to create hiding places for animals such as newts.

5 A ramp or a shallow edge to help animals access the water.

6 Rainwater for filling and topping up the pond (tapwater can contain nutrients that feed algae, which you don't want).

WILDLIFE VISITORS TO EXPECT

Your pond will attract a variety of different animals:

7 Common frogs eat slugs, snails, worms, and insects; their skin dries out in heat or strong wind, so provide shelter near the pond.

8 Common toads eat slugs, spiders, and insects; they need deeper water than frogs to lay their eggs, but can live in drier places.

9 Little brown bat species eat only insects; it has been said that these creatures can eat up to 1,000 insects in a single night.

10 Many birds feed huge quantities of insects to their young, particularly during spring before fruits and seeds have formed.

11 Hedgehogs, and other small mammals such as opossums and skunks, eat slugs, beetles, caterpillars, earwigs, and millipedes; they need a dry place to shelter and plenty of space to roam.

12 Common newts eat slugs and insects; they need narrow-leaved submerged plants to lay their eggs on.

A HAVEN FOR WILDLIFE

To attract the greatest number of predators, design a natural-looking wildlife pond with a shallow edge, to give birds and amphibians plenty of entry points. Plant the edges with a good variety of moisture-loving plants to provide shelter for the wildlife.

The Healing Garden

Introduction

Your garden can be a healer, reducing stress and pain, refreshing tired minds, boosting immunity, and creating space for quiet contemplation.

A raft of scientific evidence reports that spending even a short time in nature is vital for human health, promoting both physical and mental well-being. Gardening can boost self-esteem and help us to connect with others, while the repetitive patterns in nature fascinate us, relaxing and rebooting the brain. Scented plants can have unique healing qualities and plant color affects our emotions—learn how you can use these features to create a healing and therapeutic garden. The sound and sight of water has the power to calm and relax us, and a water feature is especially effective for attracting birds and their soothing birdsong to your garden. Your healing garden has other benefits, too. Gardening can strengthen your immune system by exposing you to beneficial soil microbes, and studies show that not only are outdoor activities such as gardening good exercise, but they can potentially help to slow the aging process as well.

Feel good with Vitamin G

Urban environments can negatively affect our physical and mental health, but "Vitamin G" can be the antidote.

Several studies show that immersing ourselves in nature, or even just looking at it, is good for our mental and physical health. Nature has such a life-enhancing effect on us that some researchers have likened it to a vitamin—Vitamin G (Green)—that our bodies need to function well, and recommend we take a daily dose. Pilot designs in the UK even suggest that a prescription of gardening or walking in nature can be more beneficial in treating some disorders, such as high blood pressure and depression, than conventional medicines.

A LACK OF GREEN IS BAD FOR US

Green spaces—from remote wilderness to city parks and gardens—are fast disappearing, and there's mounting evidence that it's not good for us. Just as diminishing habitats threaten the survival of other animals on Earth, our disconnection from nature and green spaces is linked to a rise in depression, anxiety, heart disease, obesity, low immunity, and even some types of cancer.

Many of us lack vital exposure to greenery. In one survey, **1 in 10 children** in the UK had **not visited a natural space in 12 months**; that proportion grew within low-income groups.

Dangers of disconnection

A host of research studies has examined the health problems associated with a lack of exposure to nature, or "nature-deficit disorder." Studies such as those in Germany and the Netherlands in the 2010s, for example, have shown that spending most of our time either surrounded by buildings or indoors negatively affects our physical and mental well-being. A study of more than 340,000 people in the Netherlands revealed that people living without

Research suggests that a **lack of exposure** to green spaces **increases the incidence of attention and mood disorders**, such as attention deficit disorder (ADD) in children.

A study of **3,000 Japanese citizens age 74** and above found that **access to green**, walkable paths and spaces significantly **increased their life expectancy**. Studies of older people in the UK found similar results.

easy access to a green area were 33 percent more likely to suffer from depression and 44 percent more likely to be affected by anxiety disorders than those living within walking distance of a park or other natural environment Some researchers believe that in poorer urban areas, a lack of nature may even contribute to the higher incidence of mental and physical health complaints suffered by residents.

As evidence on the harmful effects of urban living stacks up, scientists and pressure groups are calling for change.

Getting back to green

While living in "gray" areas is damaging to our health, exposure to green brings numerous benefits. A 1991 study showed that exposure to nature lowered stress and anxiety, improving mood and lowering blood pressure and heart rate. Other research indicates that being in nature is mentally restorative, allowing us to focus better. Research in Europe, the United States, and Australia consistently provides further evidence for the power of Vitamin G.

Health professionals are also now tuning in to the "green is good" philosophy. Therapists in the UK, for instance, use horticultural programs to treat a range of physical and mental health conditions, including anxiety and post-traumatic stress disorders. Marginalized groups, such as young offenders, report increased feelings of self-worth and belonging while engaged in these programs. In the business world, staff retention levels and productivity are higher in workplaces that maintain gardens or keep indoor plants. So how can you get *your* dose of Vitamin G?

A study of hospital patients revealed the **healing effect of nature**. Those with a window view of a **natural setting** healed faster and **needed fewer analgesics** than patients with a view of a brick wall.

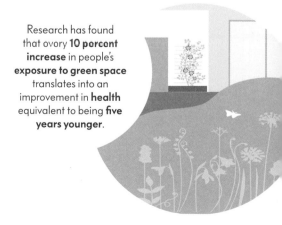

Research has found that every **10 percent increase** in people's **exposure to green space** translates into an improvement in **health** equivalent to being **five years younger**.

GETTING YOUR DOSE OF VITAMIN G

Studies show that one of the **main benefits** of spending time in **nature** is **reduced stress levels**

You cannot overdose on Vitamin G. Research shows that the more you get, the better, and a study published in 2019 suggested that even two hours of "green time" a week can be beneficial. Use your local green area as a therapeutic space, whether it's a nearby park or woods, a garden on your doorstep, or a balcony covered in plants.

Daily dose

You don't even have to go outside or have a garden to boost your Vitamin G levels. Simply looking at nature through a window will increase your intake. Gazing at a natural scene for just five minutes can alleviate symptoms of stress and anxiety, lowering blood pressure and reducing the heart rate. Make sure you can see green spaces from your home and find excuses to be in your outside space, even if just for a short time each day. Incorporate nature into your everyday life by walking through parks as part of a daily commute. In winter you'll get the same benefits, so try to look at or be in nature every day, whatever the season.

For larger doses of Vitamin G, spend whole days immersed in nature. A host of studies has shown that walking in forests is particularly beneficial for physical and mental health, reducing anxiety, depression, and fatigue, as well as being revitalizing.

Checklist

Boost your Vitamin G levels by connecting with green whenever you can.

LOOKING OUT

- Plan your living areas so that you have a view of green space from workspaces, such as the kitchen or your desk, and from seating areas.
- Plant a window box or grow herbs on a sunny windowsill to brighten up the view.
- Use houseplants to bring the outside in.

GETTING OUT

- If you have a garden or balcony, put plants in containers, and locate garden seating in sheltered spots to view plants all year.
- If you have space, use the garden or balcony as an outside dining area, or take a picnic to the park.
- Stroll around your garden or do some gardening—it's a great way to combine a dose of Vitamin G with exercise.
- If possible, walk through the park on the way to work, school, or the store.
- Go for a walk or bike ride in the countryside.

Every little helps—whenever you can, boost your dose of Vitamin G by feasting your eyes on nature (top left), bringing it indoors (top right), walking through your local green spaces (far right), and enjoying your garden (right).

Willow is the perfect tree under which to position a quiet seating area—its weeping habit creates a curtain of privacy

Tall grasses, such as *Molinia* and *Miscanthus* (left), are easy to see through when walking in the garden, but provide a subtle, translucent screen when seated. They are a great way to discreetly separate the garden into different zones, and create a beautiful soothing effect as they sway in the breeze.

Submerge a seating area to provide an extra layer of seclusion

Designing a secluded haven

A secluded or semisecluded seating area can provide a peaceful place for people who suffer from anxiety, but all of us can benefit from spending time in our own company, pausing in our busy lives to relax, reflect, and contemplate.

The trick is to create a tranquil, private zone within a garden without completely shutting it off from the rest of the space. Hedges, trees, planting, and some hard structures can all be used to partially enclose or flank an inviting spot. Trees add height to a design and frame views within the garden, while mid-level planting can function as discreet screens, giving people privacy when they are seated.

Set a seating area against the boundary rather than floating in the middle of the space—solid walls or hedges offer a sense of security. Here, a screen of *Calamagrostis* x *acutiflora* 'Karl Foerster' and agapanthus add to the privacy.

Raise the crown of trees to benefit from the shade of their canopy but also to open up enticing views.

How your garden helps to reboot your brain

A connection with nature is vital for good mental health, and even the smallest garden can help calm a stressed mind.

We were all born connected to nature. Despite the internet, 24-hour news cycles, and an "always-on" pace of life today, on a primal level, our brains are still hardwired to the natural world. Scientists believe this is because instinct says nature offers rewards, like food, water, and shelter. Others suggest that we relax in gardens because we associate them with restoration and they make few demands on overtaxed brains. Whatever the reason, certain botanical feaures are known to promote well-being—and you can design your own garden around them.

HOW NATURE RESTORES US

Humans are "biophiles," meaning we have an innate affinity with the natural world and derive emotional well-being from it, as scientific research shows. In one US study in the early 1990s, three groups of participants were asked to focus on an attentionally fatiguing task for 40 minutes. They then either went for a walk in nature or in an urban area, or read and listened to music. Those who had been in nature were able to concentrate better afterward, and reported feeling more positive and restored than other participants.

Theories of natural well-being

How and why do natural environments have such a positive impact on people? Science offers different explanations. Arousal theory of motivation, for instance, says that nature provides optimal levels of stimulation, balancing the excitement of viewing something new and complex with the calm of the naturally familiar. Perceptual fluency account states that we react more positively to natural scenes than human-made ones because we subconsciously process the repetitive patterns in nature, such as leaf or petal arrangements, more easily.

It's important to remember that the comfort offered by a natural environment depends on your own place within it. For instance, most people prefer to sit with their back against a

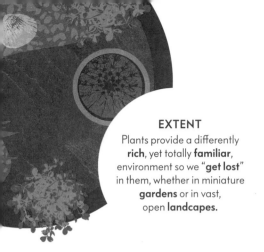

EXTENT
Plants provide a differently **rich**, yet totally **familiar**, environment so we "**get lost**" in them, whether in miniature **gardens** or in vast, open **landcapes**.

BEING AWAY
Natural scenes, no matter how small, offer a **mental break**— a chance to **escape** from daily life and **stress.**

wall, gazing out at open spaces, according to prospect-refuge theory. Your instinct to observe a landscape (prospect) from a protected vantage point (refuge) stems from an built-in desire to see approaching danger. Find this position, whether in your home or your garden, and it may help reduce your stress levels.

The ART of natural restoration

The most influential theory to date, however, is attention restoration theory (ART). Developed by environmental psychologists Stephen and Rachel Kaplan in the 1980s and '90s, it suggests that encounters with nature allow us to rest, reflect, and restore our overworked minds—all of which are vital to good health, and improve our ability to focus and perform effectively back in the increasingly gray, urban world.

According to ART, a restorative environment must offer these four elements: a sense of total immersion ("**extent**"), a change of scene ("**being away**"), a feeling of being at ease within your environment ("**compatibility**"), and features that hold your attention ("**fascination**"). Natural settings like these let your mind recover from the relentless mental processing that modern life demands, restoring your well-being.

As a gardener, you have the opportunity to create a truly restorative natural environment in any space, inside or out, by including design features and plants with sensory qualities that resonate with, and help reboot, your brain.

COMPATIBILITY
Our **instinctive affinity** with **nature** means that we immediately feel **calmer** and more at **ease** in a **natural setting** than in an artificial, human-made one.

FASCINATION
The **natural world** is filled with **intriguing** objects—leaves, flowers, snowflake patterns— that gain our **attention**, but in an effortless, almost **meditative** way. Patterns known as **fractals** (see p.72) occupy our brain with "**soft fascination**" but make no demands upon it.

HOW NATURE FASCINATES

Watch a sunset, gaze at an ocean, or simply look out at your garden. As you view the changing sky, the ebb and flow of waves, or plants swaying in the breeze, time seems to slow. Your breathing deepens, your heart rate decreases, stressful thoughts recede. You may feel calmer. This, according to ART (see p.71), is because nature is rebooting your brain.

Nature captures our attention with repetitive patterns, known as fractals. Fractals are found in plants, animals, and landscapes—almost everywhere, in fact, in the natural world. The arrangement of tree branches, the anatomy of snowflakes, clouds, leaf patterns, even your own heart rhythm—all exhibit fractals. Research says we're drawn to these patterns because they're easy to process, and looking at them gently takes the brain "offline," allowing it to recover.

The perfect pattern

Not all fractals are created equal: too complex, and they're confusing; others fail to engage us at all. UK and Swedish researchers, however, found which pattern types draw our attention most effectively: we respond best to natural features that are moderately complex: neither too smooth and sparse, nor too intricate and dense. A grassy landscape that combines open views with some trees is ideal: the scene's silhouette contains the patterns with which we have the most affinity.

Some of the most compelling fractals also reflect a mathematical proportion known as the Fibonacci sequence, in which each number in the sequence equals the sum of the two numbers preceding it. The spiral arrangement of pine cones and centers of sunflowers show this ratio, as do snail shells and some seashells.

So, remember the science when designing your garden. The flat, hard landscaping you might have had in mind will need the fascinating fractals of a tree, some shrubs, and a flower border to be truly restorative.

How fractals work

Visual repetition is key to how and why fractals fascinate us. Designs that repeat themselves in a particular ratio hold our attention, tempting it to follow the pattern to its end—especially when the pattern recurs at different sizes in a seemingly endless progression. For example, many trees fork from a central main trunk into branches, which then fork into other branches. This branching continues, repeating from large to small, right down to the tiniest twig.

Twigs, branches, and trunk follow a similar repeating branching pattern

The geometry of attraction

Fractals occur in all flowers, but we are naturally attracted to some more than others. Research shows that humans consistently prefer radially symmetrical flowers, such as sunflowers, particularly those whose parts are arranged in a spiral around a central axis. This fractal holds and restores our attention, possibly because of the fact that if the flower is divided along several different planes or sight lines, each half is still symmetrical. Flowers such as orchids, however, aren't as appealing. They are bilaterally symmetrical: they can be divided equally along only one plane, thus scoring lower on the "fascination scale."

Fractals are found throughout nature, such as the patterns made by dahlia petals (top left), the spirals in an aloe (top right), and the scrolls of some young ferns (above).

A sunflower has radial symmetry, which increases its aesthetic appeal

A slipper orchid has bilateral symmetry, which is thought to decrease its aesthetic appeal

DESIGN YOUR GARDEN FOR FASCINATION

A garden for fascination needs to combine optimal interest with mind-calming benefits. First, examine your garden's overall shape. Where do the areas of most interest lie?

Do your eyes naturally move to a particular point, such as a flower bed? Any sightlines should really capture your attention and draw you easily into the space. Most natural shapes are curved, which is why a straight row of flat, concrete paving slabs to the back fence won't be nearly as inviting as a winding stone or brick pathway, possibly interplanted with fragrant groundcover herbs to soften the hard edges. Consider introducing some additional organic shapes into your garden landscape, because we tend to find forms that mimic nature more fascinating to contemplate.

Blur boundaries to increase space

Create intrigue by hiding some areas with screens, trees, or hedges—spaces glimpsed through an opening invite exploration. Soften any boundaries with shrubs, climbers, or trees, which will disguise walls or fences and, in turn, make your garden feel larger.

Try using houseplants to link your interior and exterior spaces. Position foliage, flowers, or shapes that echo those in the garden near windows, and your indoor plants will naturally lead your eye to their counterparts outside.

Just add water

In addition to offering a natural focal point and a resource for wildlife, water makes a natural meditative focal point—perfect for a quiet corner to reboot (see pp.78–79). A small pond (see p.112) or birdbath will reflect seasonal skies and scudding clouds, drawing your eye to these ephemeral images. If you have space, add a softly splashing fountain or a rill; its gentle trickling will soothe a tired mind (see p.113).

Any water feature, from a simple bowl to a large pond, will engage the eye with its movement or the action of water rippling in the breeze.

A pathway that leads to a destination, such as a bench or sculpture, will encourage you to move through the space.

Key features to include in your garden

- Visual pathway through the space
- Water features
- Areas that invite exploration
- Elements of intrigue and interest along sight lines

Repeating shapes, such as these round box shrubs, create fascination by drawing the eye in and around the space, and their curved forms are pleasing to us, too.

PLANT YOUR GARDEN FOR FASCINATION

Once you've planned your garden, it's time to fill it with plants that offer maximum "soft fascination"—those that help your mind to rest and recover. A range of planting will attract attention with shapes and fractal patterns, but some plants are more fascinating than others.

Plant for interest and balance

Include plants of various shapes and heights for intriguing contours, placing taller trees and shrubs at the back, with smaller plants in front. Build in fractal repetition (see p.72) with sets of plants of similar forms throughout, arranging them in groups (use odd numbers for a natural look) and layers that connect and flow to create your own "fascination-scape."

Balanced landscapes are those that include open spaces as well as trees, shrubs, and other plants. That's why a garden containing only lawn or paving provides very little fascination, yet one so jammed with plants that it lacks open areas is too confusing to be a place of calm.

It is equally important to keep balance in mind when it comes to plant choices. Select those with leaves and flowers made up of fractal patterns and you're well on your way to creating a garden that reboots your brain. The textured or patterned leaves of arums and ferns (see opposite) have a familiar and calming shape, as well as enough intricate details to hold your gaze. The radial symmetry (see p.73) of daisy- or saucerlike flowers, including zinnias (see opposite) and cosmos, makes them ideal too.

A garden for all senses

Ideally, restorative gardens should fascinate *all* the senses: sight, smell, hearing, touch, even taste, if you plant edibles. Scientific research shows that scent has a direct impact on our emotional well-being (see p.92), so include fragrant flowering plants known to be calming or mood-elevating, such as lavender, damask rose, and jasmine. Grasses that rustle in the breeze (see opposite) create soothing "white noise," as well as offering feathery stems to run your fingers through. Many flowers also attract bees and other pollinators (see p.194), which add sensory layers of sight and sound.

Plant for all seasons

Evergreens guarantee some winter interest, but mix these with deciduous plants and you'll set a scene that shifts and changes, offering spring blossom through to fall leaf color. The key is to create a succession of star turns; bare branches dusted with frost provide fascination in winter, but those same branches can be equally fascinating in full summer leaf.

PLANTS THAT FASCINATE

Include a range of plants with contrasting colors and features, blending intricate leaf patterns with attractive blooms to maximize the opportunities to bring fascination into your garden. Here are some suggestions, but remember to look for plants that will thrive in your climate and soil type.

1 Mexican feather grass (*Stipa tenuissima*) This deciduous perennial appeals to the eye with its movement, and also to the ear with a soft rustling in the wind.

2 Zinnia (*Zinnia elegans*) This annual combines fractal complexity with the radial symmetry of its daisylike blooms.

3 Italian arum (*Arum italicum*) The varigated leaves of this perennial have intriguing patterns to engage the eye and hold our attention.

4 Male fern (*Dryopteris filix-mas*) The classic fractal leaf structures of this deciduous plant engage effortless attention, restoring the mind.

5 Foxglove (*Digitalis obscura*) A biennial or short-lived perennial, its flowers have intricate patterns that draw the gaze with their gentle complexity, and it attracts bumblebees, whose buzzing adds a soothing layer of sound.

MAKE A MINDFULNESS CORNER

Mindfulness is the practice of focusing on the present while acknowledging—but not being overwhelmed by—thoughts and emotions. A form of meditation, it is encouraged by health professionals to help with conditions such as anxiety and depression, but can aid anyone seeking peace of mind. If you're designing your garden to reboot your brain, making a mindfulness corner helps to enhance that effect.

Position your zone in a quiet corner, perhaps near the soothing sounds of water. Your garden refuge allows your mind to rest in a safe, peaceful space.

Choose a safe space

To feel truly calm, you need to feel secure and removed from distractions, so a sheltered, out-of-the-way corner makes an ideal mindfulness site. Place a comfortable seat with its back to a wall, fence, or hedge to foster a sense of security (see p.71), then partially enclose the space with vegetation to filter out buildings or street areas, as well as any anxieties associated with them. You can do this in a garden or on a balcony.

Tune in to nature

Include water (see p.110) and plant nectar-rich flowers around your seating to lure bees, butterflies, and other pollinators to your mindfulness zone. Their movements and gentle buzzing sounds will engage your senses and help you to focus on the present. Surround your space with green and flowering plants with patterns and colors that please you, such as vibrant penstemons or more muted achilleas; their shades and shapes will ground you in the present as your brain processes their complexity. Look out, too, for architectural seedheads, such as alliums (see below), and vivid colors, such as the dazzling pink and turquoise of glory flowers.

Choose plants whose scents (see p.92) you enjoy and engage your sense of touch by selecting tactile plants such as lamb's ears (see below), so you can stroke the soft, velvety leaves. Add some lavender (see below), rosemary, or your particular favorite fragrant plants to stimulate your sense of smell. A fascinating sensory corner that offers the soothing benefits of mindfulness will give you the ultimate brain reboot.

SENSORY GARDEN STARS

Mindfulness involves tuning in to the present, partly by engaging the senses, so when designing your garden corner, choose plants with sensory qualities that appeal to you.

1 Alliums (*Allium* 'Purple Sensation') Globes of bright color, which give way to a display of pincushion seedheads, catch your eye with their fascinating forms.

2 Lavender (*Lavandula*) A calming, aromatic scent engages your sense of smell, helping you to be in the moment.

3 Lamb's ears (*Stachys byzantina*) Soft, tactile leaves stimulate your sense of touch whenever you brush against them.

Designing your seating

Taking time to enjoy relaxing in your garden will offer maximum benefit to your physical and mental well-being, and in order to do so, a well-considered choice of seating is essential. Do not limit yourself to just one seated area; gardens should be enjoyed from multiple locations and, in most cases, there should be space for this. A simple backless bench may offer a moment's pause, while a low-level armchair could be placed somewhere you can settle into. Choose furniture that suits the lifestyle you lead, not the one you wish you had, and you will be more likely to get out and enjoy the garden.

Revealing a hint of a bench is a simple way to create intrigue and a desire to want to explore the garden, while a seat positioned under trees or surrounded by hedging can feel secure and relaxing.

Planting closely against seating can create a truly immersive experience and encourage peaceful interaction with nature. Here, I've planted hostas, *Brunnera macrophylla* 'Jack Frost', *Liriope*, foxgloves, and *Dryopteris* as a harmonious backdrop to the bench.

Flank a seating area with trees to create a cozy sense of enclosure and provide dappled shade on hot, sunny days. I used multi-stemmed cherry for its striking architectural form, high canopy to allow views through the garden, and the beautiful burst of blossom in the spring

Organic forms and meandering paths encourage you to amble slowly through your garden to a seating area. Fringing the path here are plantings of Siberian flag iris, *Nepeta racemosa* 'Walker's Low', *Camassia*, and *Salvia*.

CREATE A BRAIN-BOOSTING INDOOR GARDEN

If you have no garden or outside space, or spend most of your daylight hours inside, you can still create your own healing garden indoors. A wealth of scientific research shows that having plants in interior spaces improves concentration levels, elevates mood, and lowers stress and blood pressure levels. In fact, one UK study conducted in 2014 found that enriching a previously spartan space with plants increased the workers' overall productivity by 15 percent. Indoor plants can also cleanse the air of toxins and alter relative humidity, which improves your health and comfort—and when you feel better physically, your mental state naturally improves.

Match the plant to the space...

While it's clear that indoor plants help to reboot your brain, what is the best way to maximize their benefits? First, when choosing plants for your home or office, opt for types that will thrive in your particular space. If a room does not receive a lot of natural light, pick a leafy shade-lover, such as the Chinese evergreen or ZZ plant. Succulents and cacti flourish in hot, sunny sites, such as south-facing windowsills, while most orchids, other flowering plants, and some patterned foliage plants enjoy a bright room but not direct sunlight.

...and the color to the mood

Think about the function of the room in question, as both foliage and flower colors can affect the ambience (see p.100). A 2013 study in Japan showed that while dark-green plants make a space feel more relaxed and calm, red plants aid intense concentration. Brighter greens and yellows can enhance energy levels.

Keep fascination in mind

By grouping plants of different shapes, shades, species, and sizes, you'll replicate the fascination aspects of natural landscapes (see pp.70–73) so beneficial to well-being. Also use windows as that crucial "open space" referred to in prospect refuge theory (see p.71). A 2005 study showed that positioning plants near windows helps to lower human stress levels even more by drawing our eyes to them and to the view beyond—the brain is relaxed by looking at distant landscapes.

Even when space is at a premium, there are easy ways to help reboot your brain with greenery. A spider plant by a window is visually fascinating, and the views through the window can lower stress.

Plants to fascinate

Populate your indoor garden with houseplants that provide fascination with their shape, texture, and color.

- **Boston fern** (*Nephrolepis exaltata* 'Bostoniensis') forms a fountain of arching green fronds.
- **ZZ plant** (*Zamioculcas zamiifolia*) bears fronds of mid-green glossy leaflets arranged in pairs.
- **Dragon** (*Dracaena marginata*) has sprays of sword-shaped, gently curving striped leaves.
- **Snake plant** (*Sansevieria trifasciata*) features long, leathery, architectural green leaves that are often attractively marbled.
- **Echeverias** (*Echeveria* spp.) form elegant, textural rosettes in a range of colors.

An interesting mix of green plants with intriguingly shaped and patterned leaves will help to take your mind "offline," creating a soothing indoor refuge to help you to restore, relax, and reboot.

How gardening can boost your self-esteem

Gardening helps you grow more than just plants—it can also increase confidence levels and feelings of self-worth.

That feeling of pride you get when your garden flourishes, or your first seedlings come through, is a powerful positive emotion. Caring for a green space has been proven to foster a sense of ownership, control, connection, and responsibility—and research shows that these reactions increase self-confidence, making us feel more positive about ourselves.

CONTROL BUILDS CONFIDENCE

People suffering from stress or depression often say they feel powerless to change their situation, but gardening offers a promise of control— tending a green space, making planting choices, following the rhythms of the seasons, connecting to a little patch of nature. You don't have to own a garden; even a balcony can bring benefits, and joining a community garden will create connections (see pp.90–91) and build self-esteem. Studies also show that gardening can be especially effective for those who may not be able—or may not *feel* able—to achieve successes in other areas of their lives.

The rewards of labor

Watching nature in action, sowing seeds, and giving plants life can be a positive, satisfying experience. Nurturing plants brings a sense of fulfillment and progression as plants grow and develop, and research shows that reaping the rewards of those labors makes people feel more confident about their abilities. Then there's the

Gardening has huge self-esteem benefits for people with **mental** or **physical disabilities**, enabling them to grow their own **food** and **flowers**, and to be **active**.

Studies show that gardening gives **older people** a sense of **purpose** and **positivity** and reduces feelings of **isolation**.

Many studies show that being in a garden or green space **elevates mood** and **feelings of self-worth** for those suffering with **anxiety** or **depression**.

physical benefits of keeping fit through active gardening (see pp.126–129), which also helps to boost mental health and improve mood, and the positive impact of being outdoors (see pp.64–67). These rewards transcend age, social background, and gender.

Connecting through gardening

Identifying as a gardener feeds into social identity theory too, which suggests that the way we view ourselves depends on the groups we belong to. Showing like-minded friends our accomplishments in the garden not only gives us a sense of pride, but also helps to create bonds over planting or design choices, making us feel connected and less isolated (see pp.90–91).

Gardening has been proven to help give people confidence when transitioning to a new location, or even a different country. Again, it comes down to control, while also imprinting a sense of individuality: by including plants and features that remind them of their former home and creating a personal space, people can more easily assimilate into life in a new place. A 2010 study of Chinese immigrants to New Zealand, for instance, found that creating a garden helped them to "feel at home" when starting a new life in a different country, forging a sense of self and place.

Cultivating character

Psychologists believe that gardening goes beyond the immediate confidence boost, as it improves mental health by allowing us to express our own identity. They suggest that it offers a means of achieving individuality, which makes us feel competent and in control. An activity such as growing our own food, for example, can make us feel useful, that we are doing something meaningful, while working in tune with the seasons. Personalizing a space makes it unique and an expression of our own character and individuality, all of which fosters a sense of ownership and self-esteem.

Use your green space to build your own little patch of confidence-boosting paradise by setting yourself up to succeed (see pp.86–87) and personalizing your space to stamp your own character on it (see pp.88–89).

Studies show that **children** who have regular **contact with nature** have greater feelings of **self-worth** than their peers.

CHOOSE WHAT WORKS FOR YOU

So, how do you harness the ability of your green space to boost your self-esteem? How do you make sure your plants flourish and succeed, so that you can feel in control and competent?

Set yourself up to succeed

If you're relatively new to gardening, begin with reliable, easy performers such as hardy geraniums or radishes, for example, and if you are growing vegetables, make sure you choose things that you actually enjoy eating. Don't be afraid to ask for advice from your local gardening club—remember the self-worth boost that comes from feeling that you have connections and belong to a group.

When choosing your plants, look for different heights, colors, and year-round interest. And don't think you need to make it all happen overnight. Take your time and play—you're in control. If you need some inspiration, there are many plants that are quite forgiving and reliably hardy (see opposite). As you gain experience, try experimenting with more challenging crops and plants or complex projects.

Ground yourself in reality

Don't let ambition lead you astray when you're creating your perfect green space. What you have in your head has to match not only the practicalities of your soil type and climate, but also the realities of your lifestyle and time commitments. Think about what you want from your space and how much time you will have to tend it. If your garden is going to bolster your self-esteem, it cannot be the thing you're constantly feeling guilty about because you're behind on your gardening tasks.

Work with what you have

In a courtyard garden, on a balcony, or if you live in a rental, you can grow your garden in pots. Plenty of flowers, shrubs, crops, and even some trees will happily grow in containers if you feed and water them regularly. If you have limited time to tend them, an automatic irrigation system and slow-release feed can do a lot of the work for you.

There also many benefits to creating an indoor garden. Maintaining well-tended houseplants is confidence-boosting, too. You could make a mini indoor garden of cacti and succulents, which are extremely resilient and easy for new gardeners. Or try a spider plant or umbrella plant in a room with less light.

Golden rules

- Choose plants that will thrive in your space, soil, and climate—don't try to fight nature.
- Make a list of your chosen plants before going to the garden center to avoid expensive mistakes.
- Allow space for your plants to grow, rather than crowding them in.

Growing your own food is great for your self-esteem—try easy-to-grow radishes to add to crunchy salads.

The delicate flowers of Japanese anemones appear in summer and last into fall, their vigorous growth and height creating a beautiful display in a garden or on a balcony.

Plant cacti and succulents of different heights, shapes, and colors for an indoor display to be proud of.

EASY OUTDOOR PLANTS

Choose from the following plants— they are all reliable performers and ideal for new gardeners.

ORNAMENTALS

- **Japanese anemone** (*Anemone* x *hybrida*)
- **Sunflower** (*Helianthus annus*)
- **Hosta** (*Hosta*)
- **Sweet pea** (*Lathyrus odoratus*)
- **Nasturtium** (*Tropaeolum*)
- **Jerusalem sage** (*Phlomis fructicosa*)
- **Coneflower** (*Echinacea*)
- **Succulents**

FRUIT AND VEGETABLES

- **Radish** (*Raphanus sativus*)
- **Green beans** (*Phaseolus vulgaris*)
- **Swiss chard** (*Beta vulgaris*)
- **Zucchini** (*Cucurbita pepo*)
- **Strawberry** (*Fragaria* x *ananassa*)
- **Thornless blackberry** (*Ribes fruticosus*)

Sweet peas are the perfect plant for a confidence boost—they are easy to grow and will reward you with colorful, scented flowers in summer.

CALM AND CONTEMPORARY
Drawing upon influences from eastern Asia, smooth, organic shapes and clean, angular lines contrast with the irregular outlines of *Pinus sylvestris* 'Watereri', dwarf mountain pine, and yew to create a serene balance in this minimalist garden. Design by Matt Keightley.

Gardening to overcome isolation

Making connections with people through gardening can alleviate loneliness—and even help you to live longer.

Scientists have found that the more connections you make with others, the healthier you are and the longer you're likely to live, so overcoming loneliness and making social connections is potentially the key to living a long, healthy life. Increasingly, health professionals are recognizing that gardening can be the perfect vehicle for people to connect. Research shows that those who belong to a gardening group or who tend a community garden feel less isolated and enjoy better physical and mental well-being.

FINDING COMMON GROUND

Many psychologists believe that our health depends on a number of key factors, and feelings of belonging come right after our need for food, water, and shelter. Studies show that loneliness can have negative effects on physical and mental health, even affecting life expectancy. A study of more than 16,800 US citizens age 25 years or older showed that feelings of loneliness contributed to a higher risk of mortality.

Research points to isolation as a factor in raised blood pressure and higher cholesterol levels, which can lead to heart disease. This may, in part, explain why those who are isolated suffer from poorer health than people who feel connected to family or their local community.

Other research links the higher stress levels experienced by people who are isolated with lower immunity and chronic inflammation—conditions that can, in turn, expose us to more illnesses. Scientists also believe that our health can be compromised when we have no one on hand to offer emotional support or help us with day-to-day problems.

Studies have found that up to 20 percent of general practitioners' time is spent on problems caused by social issues, such as loneliness and isolation. In response, doctors have started prescribing gardening as a way of alleviating the depression and anxiety caused by isolation.

Gardening for recovery

Social and therapeutic horticulturists and horticultural therapists help people to recover from, or cope with, a range of illnesses and disabilities through gardening programs. Horticultural therapists run group and individual gardening activities, helping participants to deal more effectively with their problems.

Some programs support those with attention deficit disorder (ADD) and post-traumatic stress disorder (PTSD), using nature-based activities to increase feelings of well-being and, in some cases, aid rehabilitation and recovery. The skills participants learn can also bring a sense of belonging and job opportunities. One program designs gardens set within spinal injury units at hospitals, offering a space for patients to take part in gentle rehabilitation activities in an outdoor setting. Similar programs are offered to those who have suffered a brain injury.

Gardening for community

A 2016 study of the health and well-being benefits of community gardening in the UK, and other research, shows how community gardens can connect people from different socioeconomic, cultural, and religious groups, as well as help to integrate those who feel socially excluded. These green spaces are neutral territory, literally providing an area of common ground for people of quite different backgrounds to discuss growing techniques, share and compare knowledge, exchange skills, seeds, and plants, and work together to grow food, flowers, and resilient communities. A practical shared focus such as this can build life-enhancing connections and friendships.

Join a community garden program and benefit from the invaluable human connections that can build your confidence and gardening knowledge.

Get involved

Community garden programs take place around the world, so get in touch with local groups to see what they can offer. You will meet a wide variety of people, share new skills, and build connections with others in your local neighborhood. Alternatively, you could get involved by introducing children to gardening at a nearby school. By incorporating gardening into the curriculum, school programs enhance children's life skills, such as teamwork and confidence, and build on their literacy, science, and numeracy learning.

The powerful impact of scent

Fragrance can have a potent and emotive influence on us, but it can also have therapeutic qualities.

For centuries, people have believed in the power of botanical scents to boost mood, health, and well-being. Scientific studies are now providing increasing evidence for the effects on us of plant scents, showing that the parts of the brain that process smell, memory, and emotion are closely related, and that scents can affect our brainwaves in powerful ways. Cultivate scented plants throughout the seasons to create a natural therapeutic garden that will boost your well-being all year round.

SCENTS ON THE BRAIN

A person takes about 23,000 breaths a day, and some studies suggest that we can detect more than 1 trillion odors. This impressive ability has likely contributed to humans' successful evolution, as we are attracted to "good" smells present in sources helpful to survival, and repelled by scents from potentially harmful sources, such as rotten food or smoke.

We perceive odors when molecules in the air we breathe attach to receptor cells in the nose. Information is processed by olfactory bulbs, and then sent to the brain. Our first association with an odor is thought to be "locked" into the brain, and predicts our reaction when we next encounter the same smell.

Scents can also unlock powerful memories and seem to evoke more personal and emotionally intense memories than stimuli from the other senses. Researchers suspect that this is because the parts of the brain that process our experiences of scent have strong links to associative learning, emotions, and short- and long-term memories.

The **human nose** contains about **400** different types of **olfactory receptors**, which detect **odors** in **concentrations** as low as **1 part** per **30 billion**.

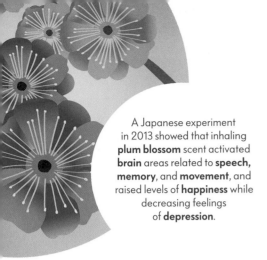

A Japanese experiment in 2013 showed that inhaling **plum blossom** scent activated **brain** areas related to **speech, memory**, and **movement**, and raised levels of **happiness** while decreasing feelings of **depression**.

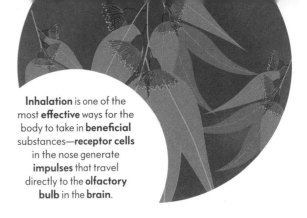

Inhalation is one of the most **effective** ways for the body to take in **beneficial** substances—**receptor cells** in the nose generate **impulses** that travel directly to the **olfactory bulb** in the **brain**.

that plays a key role in emotion and memory. Research into plant oils suggests that certain plants' scents have the potential to affect us physiologically and mentally, improving mood, increasing alertness, reducing stress and anxiety, improving memory, and even reducing blood pressure.

The science of scent

Scent is significant in the botanical world. Plants generate odors to lure pollinators, attract animals to eat fruits and disperse seeds, and to ward off predators. But why do different plant scents have different effects on people?

Science is only starting to find answers, but studies show that scents affect brainwaves in measurable ways. Evidence increasingly supports the role of lavender scent in cognitive performance, as a mood and sleep aid, muscle-relaxant, and migraine reliever. While this may

in part be due to its pleasant odor leading to a positive emotional response, evidence also suggests physiological effects, including the scent interacting with brain receptors and neurotransmitters to promote relaxation. Rosemary, which has long been used in aromatherapy to boost energy levels and has traditional links with memory (see box below), has also shown to suppress both beta and alpha brainwaves, which increases alertness and learning retention.

Design your own therapeutic garden (see pp.94–97) of plants that fill the air with their scents to enhance your well-being.

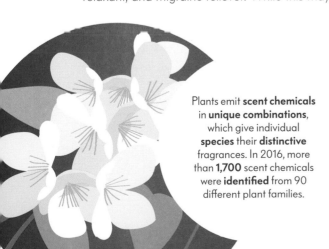

Plants emit **scent chemicals** in **unique combinations**, which give individual **species** their **distinctive** fragrances. In 2016, more than **1,700** scent chemicals were **identified** from 90 different plant families.

Rosemary to remember?

For years, rosemary's traditional link with memory was dismissed by the scientific community, but scientists are now rethinking their stance. In 2015, UK researchers tested 60 older volunteers and found that inhaling rosemary oil significantly improved their working memory: the ability to remember to do things in the future, such as mailing a letter or taking medicine. Several compounds in rosemary seem to prevent the breakdown of specific brain neurotransmitters that are necessary for working memory to function. Inhaling these compounds gets the "new" memories into the brain directly—rosemary and other plant scents could be key players in the future treatment of memory loss in dementia, or in restoring the sense of smell to people who have lost it after a brain injury.

DESIGNING YOUR SCENTED SPACE

Consider how to make the most of your space before you decide which plants to include in your aromatic garden (see pp.96–97). Think about which areas you use the most and which get the most sunlight. Heat can intensify the scent given off by the foliage of some plant types, such as pine and other conifers, as well as thyme, oregano, and other herbs that originated in the Mediterranean. If you use your garden in the evening, you may want to create a scented night garden (see pp.200–201). Most plants release scent during daylight hours, but those pollinated by nocturnal insects are most fragrant at night.

A scent for all reasons

Given the power of plants to influence our moods, think about what effects you want to create. Do you need an area solely for relaxation, or one that will invigorate you or increase concentration? If you have space, try planting different areas with different mood-enhancers so you can enjoy their specific effects whenever they are needed.

Plan to have a sequence of fragrances and include key signature scents in areas of your garden throughout the seasons. For example, winter-scenting viburnum and witch hazel are some of the sweetest perfumed plants. Enjoy the chocolate-scented flowers of *Azara*

microphylla 'Variegata' in late winter and spring, and the lemon-scented lemon verbena foliage of *Aloysia triphylla* in summer. In fall, the foliage of *Cercidiphyllum japonicum* 'Boyd's Dwarf' sends out a maltose scent of cotton candy.

Space out plants that waft scent strongly over a wide area, such as daphnes, some types of lily, and flowering tobacco, so that they don't overwhelm more subtle aromas.

At your feet

Start from the ground up. Fill any gaps between paving stones and slabs with low-growing aromatic ground-covering species such as thyme, Corsican mint, and chamomile. Fill the spaces with a mix of well-drained compost and sand and plant into this, watering well.

Plant low-growing fragrant flowers such as lily of the valley or scented violas alongside paths, or where two paths intersect, so that passing feet may brush against the plants, causing them to release more of their scent.

Contained spaces and heady scents

Group containers planted with aromatic herbs on a sunny, sheltered terrace, beside seating, or on a windowsill. Plant scented annuals and tender plants in pots or boxes close to windows, so their scent can drift indoors. Move potted lilies into gaps in the summer border so that they waft scent above the herbaceous planting.

Make the most of scented climbers, such as jasmine, growing them on arches or pergolas so that you catch their fragrance as you walk beneath. Frame seats with climbers or shrubs, so you can sit enveloped by their scent.

Fragrant ground-huggers planted between paving slabs, such as this chamomile lawn, will release their scent with light foot traffic.

Create scented zones at head height with highly fragrant plants, such as this rambling rose and honeysuckle trained over an arch.

Plant aromatic herbs, such as sage and rosemary, in pots and group them together in a sunny spot so that they release their scents in the heat of the day.

CHOOSING YOUR SCENTS

Scent is a complex mixture of chemical compounds that vaporize when they are released from a plant. Botanical scents are often described as honey-scented, lemon-scented, spicy, musky, aromatic, sweet-scented, or fruit-scented. Given that the fragrance of just one flower may contain more than 100 volatile organic compounds (VOCs)—compounds that easily become vapors—how should you go about identifying the best-smelling plants for your own garden?

Keep it personal

Very simply, if a plant smells good to you, it's a perfect candidate for your aromatic garden. While all human brains process scent in the same way, each of us (with the exception of identical twins) is born with a unique set of olfactory receptors determined by our genes. This means that you perceive odors slightly differently from anyone else on the planet.

Cultural associations, memories, and experiences also affect your scent preferences and how you respond to particular plants—and again, these are deeply personal. The scent of clematis or wisteria, for instance, might remind you of a sunny day spent with loved ones, but for someone else, it may be associated with a painful beesting, or they may be chemically sensitive to the smell (see p.46).

Remember, too, that some plants have not only scented flowers but also aromatic foliage. Rub fragrant leaves between your fingers to see how their fragrance affects you.

JASMINE
(*Jasminum officinale*)

It takes **8,000 jasmine flowers** to produce just **0.03oz (1g)** of jasmine **oil**

SCENTS FOR WELL-BEING

Studies show that certain plants have specific effects on us when we inhale their scents or their essential oils.

- **Jasmine** (*Jasminum officinale*) Its effects include enhancing sleep, improving memory, and increasing mental accuracy, vigilance, and visual awareness.
- **Chinese juniper** (*Juniperus chinensis* 'Kaizuka') Scent from the foliage has a relaxing effect.
- **Peppermint** (*Mentha* x *piperata*) Enhances attention, alertness, and memory and task performance; reduces stress.
- **Marjoram** (*Origanum majorama*) Encourages sleep and relaxation, reduces depression and anxiety.
- **Japanese apricot** (*Prunus mume*) Can improve mood and may support vital brain functions.

- **Damask rose** (*Rosa* x *damascena*) Relaxes muscles and helps to release emotional tension.
- **Clary sage** (*Salvia sclarea*) Increases feelings of happiness and counters depression, including low mood associated with the menopause and postnatal depression.
- **Valerian** (*Valeriana officinalis*) Increases the amount and quality of sleep.
- **Rosemary** (*Rosmarinus officinalis*) Enhances alertness and quality of memory, reduces anxiety, and stimulates improved mood.
- **Lavender** (*Lavandula*) Improves concentration and computational speed and accuracy, reduces stress and anxiety, increases relaxation, and improves mood.

DAMASK ROSE
(*Rosa* x *damascena*)

ROSEMARY
(*Rosmarinus officinalis*)

MARJORAM
(*Origanum majorama*)

LAVENDER
(*Lavandula*)

Designing your scented space

Scent can connect people directly to nature and the environment, and it is arguably one of the most effective features in a well-being garden. Certain fragrances have a significant and positive effect on emotions, and they can also be hugely nostalgic—cut grass in early spring marks a cheering moment of new hope in the year; relaxing drifts of lavender or heady notes of roses wafting into the house from a nearby shrub recall lazy summer days.

Consider which fragrances make you happy, help you feel calm, or stimulate you, then pick plants to evoke these emotions as you move through or sit in the garden. Many scented plants do best in full sun, so choose the sunniest spots for them. Site winter-scented plants on the approach to the front door so that you smell them as you come and go. Scent is highly personal—follow your instinct.

Use scented climbers in pairs to prolong seasonal interest and aroma. Evergreen jasmine (above) is an excellent year-round form, while wisteria (top) offers a fragrant show in spring, and often a second flowering. They enjoy the same conditions.

Scented groundcover plants such as thyme or chamomile work well in gaps in paved areas

Leave a gap between paving slabs and plant a scented groundcover between them; as your feet brush over, they will release their fragrance.

Plant a scented climber such as wisteria to waft its fragrance over seating areas

Dress a table with pots of scented flowers or herbs, such as lavender, for immediate impact

Plant herbs in pots near the house or seating area to enhance the aroma in your garden. Varying the height of the containers achieves a greater sense of depth in the space

Harnessing the power of color

Use your plants' color palette to create a display that dazzles and excites—or calms and refreshes.

Color affects our emotions, so the colors of plants we grow will have an important impact on our mood. When designing your space, think about how you want to use it and how you want to feel when you're in it. Then use color in your planting designs to help you achieve a certain mood. A design that features strong colors, such as intense reds, oranges, and yellows, will convey an exciting, lively atmosphere that is perfect for recharging. Paler colors and greens are thought to be more relaxing and calming—ideal for a mindfulness corner.

COLOR AND MOOD

Studies have shown that color has an effect on our emotions, and ongoing research has revealed that it's more than just the color, or hue, of plants that can transform our mood. In 2017, a German study found that people's emotional response to color is influenced by all three of the color dimensions: hue (true color), saturation (the purity or vividness of a color), and brightness (the degree of light a color reflects). Participants were more emotionally responsive to bright, saturated colors, for instance, than they were to darker colors with medium or low saturation.

Set the mood with your choice of color combinations. Use a mixture of plants to soften or intensify a mood, and use certain eye-catching colors in specific points of the garden to create focal points. Refer to the color wheel (see opposite) to help you design the perfect palette in your space.

The **RHS** produces a chart of **920 colors** that can be **matched** precisely to **flowers, fruits,** and **foliage** to help gardeners choose their **palette**

Bright, saturated colors are most vivid in the garden and have been shown to be the most stimulating for us to look at.

Paler, less "pure" color designs in purplish hues mixed with pale green foliage create a soothing space.

The color wheel

This wheel explains the relationship between colors. The three **primary** colors, red, yellow, and blue—pure colors that can't be obtained by mixing colors together—are at equidistant intervals around the wheel. Directly opposite each of these are **secondaries** (green, orange, and purple), a mix of two primaries. **Tertiary** colors are a mixture of adjacent primary and secondary colors.

Combining a primary with its opposite (complementary) color creates the strongest contrast, while selecting three colors that are evenly spaced around the wheel gives vibrancy with a more muted effect. Choose colors that are adjacent on the color wheel for a harmonious feel.

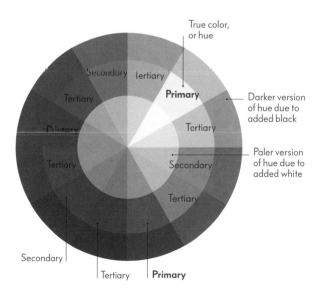

True color, or hue

Secondary Tertiary

Tertiary

Primary

Primary

Darker version of hue due to added black

Tertiary

Paler version of hue due to added white

Secondary

Tertiary

Tertiary

Secondary

Tertiary **Primary**

USING COLOR TO EXCITE

The warm hues of reds, yellows, and oranges can be combined to bring energy and intensity to planting designs, especially when bright and saturated. They can also make spaces seem smaller and create a sense of intimacy.

Dazzling reds and oranges

The eye is immediately drawn to these exciting colors, especially red, which humans find an arousing color. Use secondary or adjacent colors on the color wheel and shades of green to harmonize reds and yellows with the rest of the planting and garden. In larger spaces, use red focal points behind a more recessive color, such as green, to bring the background forward. You can also use color to attract attention to an area. Red or orange flowers at the front of a garden, or groups of red or orange plants at intervals along a border, create a color accent that will draw the eye.

Shining yellow

Although color associations are subjective, many people associate pure yellow with feelings of happiness. Use it to highlight green areas, such as lawns or shrubby borders. Plant it with its complementary color, purple, for a brightly contrasting effect. Too much yellow can be overpowering, so for a softer feel, mix shades of yellow or add neutral whites and greens.

Use different shades of a single color, such as red, to create harmony and to give a monochrome design more depth.

Color and emotion

Studies have shown that our like or dislike for particular colors is highly subjective. However, some aspects of human color preferences may be universal. For example, the ecological valence theory states that people like blues because clear sky and clean water have universal appeal, whereas browns have associations with rotting food, which prompts universal disgust. Green, the color that dominates the plant kingdom, is most positively rated across cultures, eliciting feelings of relaxation, calmness, and well-being (see pp.106–107).

Pair opposites on the color wheel—such as yellow and purple—to create a vibrant contrast.

Use three colors evenly spaced around the color wheel for drama that can be softened by using the paler, less saturated hues of secondary colors.

USING COLOR TO CALM

A design that's calming and relaxing is thought to feature colors from the cool range of the color wheel, including blue, purple, blue-purple (purple with more blue tones than red), white, and green. These, along with silver-gray foliage, such as wormwood and cotton lavender, are the typical colors of Mediterranean herb gardens and generally have a cooling effect.

Pale blues and greens are recessive colors, disappearing into the background, so use them in a design to create a sense of depth and space in small gardens. Adding pinpoints of white will bring light and freshness to the design, such as tall-stemmed flowers that tower above surrounding plants.

Relaxing blue

Threading soft blues through a planting design can give it unity as well as creating a calm and relaxing feel. Introducing darker tones, from plants with vertical forms such as agapanthus, salvias, and irises, will punctuate the planting but still create a harmonious effect. Pairing blue with orange, its complementary color, is more striking and can be used to transition from a stimulating design to a calmer one .

Purple pairings

Purple flowers grow in a wide range of shades, from the pale purple of greater periwinkle or catmint to the deep inky shade of some irises. Dark purple plants can be hard to spot in a border, especially in shady situations, so pair them with lighter companions such as acid-yellow foliage plants or white flowers to draw the eye to them. Alternatively, place them close to where you walk or sit, so that you can appreciate their dark beauty. Using several shades of purple together creates depth and intensity. A variety of flower and foliage shapes adds definition and form, helping to bring the overall effect into focus.

Add a dash of pink

Colors that are next to each other on the color wheel create a harmonious-looking planting design. Romantic designs often feature pink combined with purples and blues, with pale pink from roses and peonies, for example, providing lighter tones through the planting. Brighter, more saturated pinks, such as the magenta of Armenian cranesbill and elephant's ears, will add a touch of warmth and can make an effective transition between a cool design and a warm one.

Create a sense of space in a small area by planting recessive colors such as blue-purples and greens on the boundaries.

Frame darker colors with pale green and silver foliage to help them stand out in the planting design.

Plant adjoining colors such as different shades of purple for a harmonious combination, and use pink to add warmth.

Pair blue with orange, its complementary color, as a crossover from stimulating to tranquil designs. For a quieter display, use a less saturated orange, such as apricot.

105

Peaceful green

Green is considered a neutral color and combines well with every other hue, yet it's easy to overlook when planning your garden design. Many studies show that it's the color people find most soothing, so make it the main ingredient for areas where you want to create a feeling of calm.

There's a wide range of color variations in green, from the blue-greens of Mediterranean foliage plants and dark greens of hedging plants such as yew and holly, to the gray-greens and yellow-greens of many springtime flowers such as euphorbias. Using a selection of these different hues at varying levels of brightness and saturation will keep a predominantly green design visually interesting. Experiment with leaf sizes, textures, shapes, and forms to add interest. Large-leaved foliage plants can create scale in small spaces, especially if you don't have room for trees, and choosing evergreens ensures that there's year-round interest.

A monochrome planting can still be interesting if the leaf shapes and sizes, and plant's growing habit, are varied.

Greens for shade

Many green plants thrive in shade and are ideal for providing the framework for areas that are in shade for all or most of the day. The glistening greens of shiny-leaved shrubs and perennials draw the eye and make a great addition to shady parts of the garden. Many shade-tolerant plants have large, imposing-looking leaves, such as tree ferns and moisture-loving rodgersia, which add drama to a green scheme. Mix contrasting shapes, such as mounding plants with ones that form spires, to give definition to the design. If you need to brighten the planting,

add a sprinkling of white or cream flowers. As the evening light fades, these pale colors will glow while the greens recede. Variegated plants are useful to lighten designs in partial shade, and those with white, cream, or gold markings offer the most contrast.

Offset with green

Green shrubs and hedges such as yew and laurel can provide a dark backdrop for brighter colors, while a green lawn offsets the planting around it. Green plants threaded through a border can bring cohesion to a garden design that uses lots of different or complementary colors. They can also be restful, calming focal points planted between more attention-grabbing, intense colors. In rural gardens, green plants can provide a link to the greenery of the surrounding countryside, so that your boundaries blend with the wider landscape.

Add a hint of light and definition with variegated plants, such as hostas, to subtly widen the hues of your palette.

Constrasting shapes and heights create definition and visual interest, while the greens provide a backdrop that helps the white flowers to stand out.

CHRYSANTHEMUM
(*Chrysanthemum* 'Anastasia Green')

A RIOT OF COLOR

This glorious early-summer planting uses colors that are adjacent on the color wheel. The burnt-red irises, red verbascum, and thistlelike maroon *Cirsium* harmonize with the golden *Stipa* and melica grasses, delicate fronds of bronze fennel, and pale pink *Pimpinella*. Design by Matt Keightley.

The restorative effects of water

Water is not only soothing and calming, it also brings fascination, reflection, and light into the garden.

Blue, watery spaces can, just like green ones, help to make us feel restored, rejuvenated, and less stressed. Installing a water feature—a splashing fountain, a trickling stream, or a still pond—creates a focal point that is an endless source of calm and fascination. You don't need lots of space to enjoy the benefits of water—even a simple reflective water bowl can be a meditative feature that enhances your well-being garden.

LIVE NEAR WATER

Research shows that living near water has a positive effect on human health. One study, for example, examined the health of coastal dwellers in the UK over time. Published in 2013, it found that people who lived near the coast had significantly better general and mental health than those who lived further inland.

Living near any water—not just the sea but also lakes and rivers—can make people healther and happier, according to other research. A 2017 review of 35 studies from different countries found that the more time people spent near outdoor water, the more their mental health and well-being benefitted.

You can experience the healing powers of water with a simple water feature in your own garden. Still water, such as a large bowl or pond, can create reflections, bringing more light into the garden and adding another dimension to the setting. Moving water, such as a rill or stream, can be mesmeric and soothing, and draws the eye to different parts of the garden. The sounds of splashing water can even help to block out irritating background noises (see p.38).

We find **still** water **calming** to look at and **falling** or **flowing** water **exciting**, according to research from 2003.

In 2015, a study showed that we prefer the **sound** of **natural streams** to the sound of **fountains** and **waterfalls**.

Research in 2007 found that the **flow rate** of water is important—a **constant** flow rate may cause people to lose **interest** and so **diminish** the **restorative** effects of water over **time**.

Appearance matters: numerous studies have shown that we find **water features** more **restorative** when they look **natural**—for example, when they are an **organic shape** and there is **greenery** at the **water's edge**.

According to a 2012 study, the sound of **moving water** can make us feel **relaxed** and **drowsy** because of the **smooth** way that it rises and falls in **intensity**. This makes it a **nonthreatening sound** that can mask other, more **abrupt** noises that trigger **alert** responses.

DESIGN WITH WATER FOR WELL-BEING

No matter how small your outdoor space, you can usually find room for a simple water bowl. Placing it on the ground or sinking it into the soil draws in reflections of the sky and surrounding plants, and creates a watery surface that can become a focus for contemplation. If space is limited, you can place a small water bowl on a table. Delicate flower petals floating on the surface will add a splash of color.

To maximize reflections, make the surface area as wide as you can. Dark sides and a dark base make the reflections clearer, or you can add a black nontoxic dye to the water, which will have the same effect and will help to prevent algae growing. Obscuring the bottom of a bowl or pool also creates an illusion of depth.

Choose a material for your bowl that goes with the style of your garden. Stainless or weathered steel or copper will suit a contemporary or formal space, while cast stone or ceramic will look good in a rural or cottage garden.

Replenish the water frequently to keep it clean and clear. Use harvested rainwater rather than tap water, which can contain chemicals. A pump fitted to larger bowls and basins will keep the water clear and create the gentle sounds of moving water. For the most energy-efficient option, use a solar pump. The design of some bowls allows for the water to spill gently over the edge into a hidden reservoir, creating a moving curtain of water that is endlessly fascinating (see p.72). In others, the movement of ripples, swirls, or bubbles on the surface of the water draws the eye.

Creating calm

If you have the space, bring a sense of peace and calm into the garden with a rill (see p.114). A stone or brick rill blends in well in informal gardens; the clean lines of steel and slate suit a more contemporary space. For a small garden, a straight line makes the best use of space. In a larger garden, a more winding, organic shape allows you to conceal the full course of the rill, encouraging visitors to explore.

Even a small space can have a water feature that adds both sound and animation. A simple pump can circulate the water for a gentle and constant flow.

Falling water and green foliage create a soothing environment for this seating area. The waterlilies add visual interest and are likely to attract wildlife.

The clean, straight lines of this rill contrast with the striking foliage around it.

The gentle, trickling sounds of a rill, like a natural stream, can be soothing to tired minds. Create a gentle downward flow by placing it on a slope. Line the base of the channel with a smooth material, such as contemporary-looking cut stone or steel, to create an even flow, or use riven stone or pebbles to give the water a livelier movement and sound.

At the end of the rill, the water can either feed into a reservoir, from where a pump takes it to the top of the slope, or it can fall into a pool or trough to create the splashing sounds of a waterfall, which can help to mask unwanted noise (see p.38). Screen this lower pool with plants to introduce an element of mystery into your garden.

Reflections in a large bowl mirror the surrounding plants, enlarging the sense of space and creating an atmosphere of tranquillity.

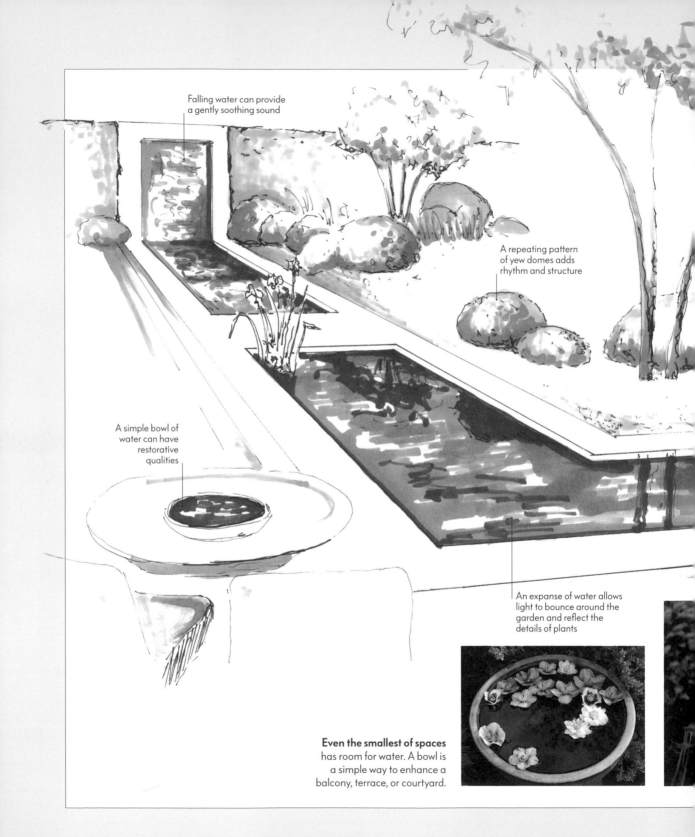

Falling water can provide a gently soothing sound

A repeating pattern of yew domes adds rhythm and structure

A simple bowl of water can have restorative qualities

An expanse of water allows light to bounce around the garden and reflect the details of plants

Even the smallest of spaces has room for water. A bowl is a simple way to enhance a balcony, terrace, or courtyard.

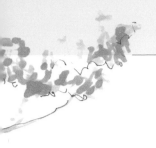

Designing your water garden

Water can enhance a space in many ways. It brings a touch of magic to the garden, an air of intrigue, and it can create myriad effects, too—reflecting sunlight, providing soothing ripples in a breeze, or introducing a gentle splashing sound that muffles unwelcome noises from beyond the boundaries of the garden.

Water is also the element that literally brings any garden to life. No sooner do you add a water feature than birds, bees, and insects will be drawn to it.

No matter how much space you have for a garden, there is a water feature to suit it. Decide what specific effect you are trying to achieve, but all will create a relaxing ambience that can transform a garden into a private sanctuary.

The luxuriant leaves of giant rhubarb contrast with the symmetrical lines of the rill

Water features offer a great opportunity to include interesting marginal plants (right), such as Siberian flag 'Purple Pansy, offset here by dwarf mountain pine.

Consider the surrounding space and how best to exploit the reflective qualities of the surface. A dark liner, stone, or nontoxic dye added to the water (left) enhances the effect.

The positive power of birdsong

Recent research shows that birdsong can relax us and help us recover from stress.

Listening to birdsong is soothing, studies show. For many of us, that may be because birdsong evokes positive associations, such as the link between birds and green spaces. Some birds' songs may be more restorative than others, and hearing a variety of birdsongs is more beneficial than hearing just one type. Turn your garden into a stress-free space by providing plenty of food, shelter, and nesting sites to make it as bird-friendly as possible.

WHY DOES BIRDSONG CALM US?

Research shows that natural sounds, in particular birdsong and moving water, have a restorative effect. In one Swedish study, volunteers completed a series of stressful tasks and listened to a particular sound after each task. The sounds included traffic, noise from a ventilation unit, a splashing fountain, and chirping birds. The volunteers' stress levels were measured by their skin conductance (how well electricity is transferred across the skin, affected by minute differences in sweat secretions). When they listened to the natural sounds, the participants' degree of stress dropped faster.

A shared history

There are several theories as to why we enjoy birdsong. Brain pathways for vocal learning in humans and birds are surprisingly similar. Evidence also indicates that human language and birdsong evolved in parallel, which may have resulted in our heightened perception and appreciation of birdsong.

Another theory as to why so many of us find birdsong relaxing is because it has pleasant associations. In studies, participants associated birdsong with nearby greenery—gardens or the countryside; with balmy weather, or being in warm seasons such as spring or summer; or

The blue tit is one of the most highly ranked birds for the restorative power of its song.

with times of day such as dawn. These associations were all generally positive. Birdsong also reminded participants of outdoor activities such as sitting in the garden or walking in the country, and many people connected birdsong with happy memories—for instance, time spent playing outside in childhood.

The more the merrier

When it comes to bird calls' positive impact, it seems that variety is better. In another Swedish study in 2014, city dwellers were asked to rate their reactions to combinations of birdsong and images of urban scenes. The results showed that participants enjoyed the singing of several bird species more than they did a single species, and that they rated urban settings more favorably when listening to birdsong.

Which birds' songs are the most restorative?

One study asked participants to what extent listening to certain bird calls would help them recover from stressful scenarios. The study used the calls of 50 birds commonly heard in the southeast of England, UK, and in New South Wales, Australia.

THE FAVORITES

The songs that listeners reported as most likely to be restorative were those that they recognized and associated with green spaces and familiar environments, such as their gardens. Birds that evoked unfamiliar environments, such as deserts, were ranked lower. Songbirds, which listeners preferred to birds with harsher calls suggestive of threat or aggression, topped the list in the study.

1 **Dunnock** (*Prunella modularis*)

2 **Greenfinch** (*Carduelis chloris*)

3 **Blackbird** (*Turdus merula*)

4 **Silvereye** (*Zosterops lateralis*) (Australian)

5 **Brown thornbill** (*Acanthiza pusilla*) (Australian)

6 **Blue tit** (*Cyanistes caeruleus*)

7 **Goldfinch** (*Carduelis carduelis*)

8 **Robin** (*Erithacus rubecula*)

9 **Wren** (*Troglodytes troglodytes*)

10 **House sparrow** (*Passer domesticus*)

Blackbird

Dunnock

Greenfinch

BRING BIRDS INTO YOUR GARDEN

If you want to benefit from the positive properties of birdsong and tap into its therapeutic potential, there are many ways to draw birds into your garden—for food, for shelter, or for nesting. Provide them with the essentials they need by putting out extra food and growing a variety of trees, shrubs, and other plants. Your planting choices, gardening habits, and even the way you plan your space can all impact on the local bird life. Many of the birds in our gardens were once woodland and hedgerow birds, but you don't need lots of space to make your garden bird-friendly—a small bird table or a bird feeder on a balcony or roof terrace can all help.

Where to put a feeder

Find the perfect spot for a bird feeder in your garden. Look for a place that is:

- **Quiet**—birds are easily scared away by human or pet activity
- **Open**—this gives birds a good view of potential predators while they are feeding
- **Sheltered**—avoid somewhere that is subjected to harsh sunlight or cold winds
- **Near a lookout**—so that birds can hide somewhere in view of the feeder, such as a small bush, to check that it's safe or wait for other birds to move on

In addition to stress-busting birdsong, attracting birds to your garden will also provide a natural pest-control service. Birds that prey on invertebrates will rid the garden of quantities of aphids, caterpillars, slugs, and even snails.

Choose plants that provide food

Birds will eat from many seed-bearing or berry-producing plants. Avoid deadheading plants and instead leave the seedheads of seed-bearing plants standing as long as possible. They will provide food for seed-eaters through the winter months.

If you are planting berry-producing plants, choose those that produce black or red berries, as these colors are easier for birds to see.

Plant flowers and long grasses to attract insects, including butterflies and moths (which produce caterpillars), that will provide plenty of prey for birds and their chicks to feed on. Even a small patch will be beneficial.

Offer extra food

You can supply extra food for birds in special feeders and on bird tables, especially in winter and spring. These extras can really make a difference to birds' survival—and even lead to growth in some bird populations. Recent research in the UK, for example, shows that regular visits to garden feeders in urban areas appear to have led to population growth across more than 30 different bird species.

Foods that birds enjoy all year round include seeds, dried fruit, and cooked rice. Suet cakes give birds an instant energy hit in winter, although some mass-produced ones are bulked out with ingredients such as husks, which aren't nutritious. If you make your own suet cakes, include seeds and nuts to offer the nutrients and antioxidants that birds need for successful breeding.

A FEAST FOR BIRDS

Plants with seedheads or berries provide food for birds, as well as interest and color in the garden.

SEEDBEARERS FOR BIRDS

1 Coneflower (*Echinacea*) The flowers attract insects, and jays, cardinals, and goldfinches all enjoy picking out the seeds from seedheads.

2 Globe thistle (*Echinops*) These purple flowers look great in the border and are particularly popular with finches.

3 Teasel (*Dipsacus fullonum*) Finches, sparrows, and buntings all eat seeds from teasel seedheads.

4 Evening primrose (*Oenothera biennis*) Leave the seedpods on the plant to ripen, and they will attract finches and siskins.

Other options
Alder (*Alnus glutinosa*), dandelion (*Taraxacum officinale*), field scabious (*Knautia arvensis*), hazel (*Corylus avellana*), hornbeam (*Carpinus betulus*), lavender (*Lavandula*)

BERRY-BEARERS FOR BIRDS

5 Holly (*Ilex aquifolium*) Songbirds, such as blackbirds, eat the berries in winter.

6 Elder (*Sambucus nigra*) The berries attract birds such as finches and robins in fall.

7 Mountain ash (*Sorbus aucuparia*) Mountain ash berries attract blackbirds and starlings.

Other options
Bird cherry (*Prunus padus*), blackthorn (*Prunus spinosa*), honeysuckle (*Lonicera periclymenum*), mistletoe (*Viscum album*), Oregon grape (*Mahonia aquifolium*)

Evergreen trees and shrubs will provide nesting sites for garden birds, such as robins, which often build nests in conifers.

Create shelter

Birds need safe places to shelter all year round. Some birds are social and will share the same tree, shrub, or climber. Others, like robins, are fiercely territorial, so if you have space, planting a variety of shrubs and trees will provide more sites. Mature trees with rough bark will attract specific woodland birds such as nuthatches and treecreepers.

Good plants for sheltering birds

Barberry (*Berberis darwinii*), false cypress (*Chamaecyparis*), Ebbinge's silverberry (*Elaeagnus* x *ebbingei*), hawthorn (*Crataegus monogyna*), holly (*Ilex aquifolium*), ivy (*Hedera helix*), honeysuckle (*Lonicera henryi*), privet (*Ligustrum vulgare*)

Provide places to nest

Many of the bird species that used to nest in holes in woodland and hedgerow trees or in old buildings now depend on gardens and other urban green spaces for their nesting sites. Installing nest boxes will encourage birds to nest in your garden (see opposite). If you have space for trees, plant sturdy specimens with plenty of branches set at an angle to provide potential sites. Climbers and shrubs that form a thick tangle of stems are also good choices and can work well in smaller gardens.

Evergreen trees, shrubs, and climbers such as honeysuckle are particularly good for birds that nest early in the year, such as robins, blackbirds, and greenfinch, as they can raise their broods out of sight from predators. Deciduous plants provide good sites for later breeders, such as finches and song thrushes. Choose thick, thorny species, such as hawthorn and barberry, which give excellent cover. Remember never to prune plants during the nesting season.

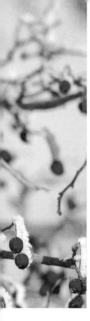

Plant hawthorn to attract birds, such as the blackbird, which eats the berries and takes refuge among the tree's thorny branches.

Put up a nest box

Nest boxes can give birds a place to roost in winter, and more nesting opportunities in spring. Birds differ in their requirements, so select the type of box that will suit the bird you want to attract. Some birds, such as wrens, need their nest to be well hidden in thick climbers, bushes, or trees, while others, such as house sparrows, don't need cover. Buy or make a nest box, ensuring that it is waterproof, made of an insulating material, such as wood or woodcrete (a mix of wood and concrete), and has a roof you can open for annual cleaning. The hole should be at least 5in (125mm) above the floor of the box to prevent predators from getting in.

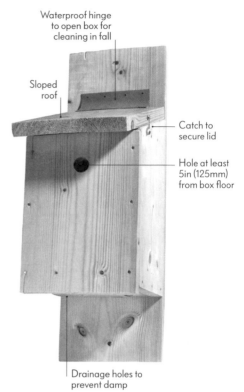

Waterproof hinge to open box for cleaning in fall

Sloped roof

Catch to secure lid

Hole at least 5in (125mm) from box floor

Drainage holes to prevent damp

Place nest boxes out of direct sunlight and protected from prevailing winds to attract birds, such as great tits, to your garden.

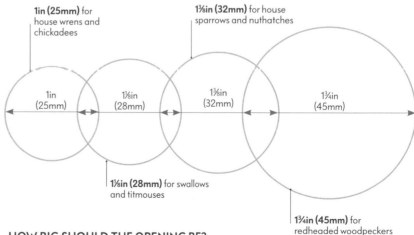

1in (25mm) for house wrens and chickadees

1⅜in (32mm) for house sparrows and nuthatches

1in (25mm)

1⅛in (28mm)

1⅜in (32mm)

1¾in (45mm)

1⅛in (28mm) for swallows and titmouses

1¾in (45mm) for redheaded woodpeckers

HOW BIG SHOULD THE OPENING BE?
Use this guide to choose the right hole size for your nest box according to the type of birds you want to attract to the garden.

Dirt is good for you

Our garden soil is full of beneficial microbes with the potential to naturally boost our immune systems.

Gardening really is good for your health. Studies show that contact with the soil gives us exposure to the beneficial microbes—microscopic organisms—that live there. These perform numerous vital functions in the body, including helping to make our immune systems more efficient. The good news is that these beneficial microbes are all around us and so we easily come into contact with them. By encouraging the whole family to get their hands in the soil, you can freely access a wide range of "good" microbes that could help keep you all healthy.

MICROBES AND OUR IMMUNITY

The human immune system works like software in a computer that needs to be fed data to perform effectively. This "data" is in the form of diverse microbes that help the immune system to identify what is a threat to the body and what can be tolerated. Humans have trillions of microbes living on or inside them—a phenomenon called the human microbiome.

We build up this microbiome by continual exposure to a range of microbes, which is why adults often have more effective immune systems than children. However, modern lifestyles mean we have less contact with these beneficial microbes, leading to a rise in auto-immune diseases, such as asthma and allergies.

Ongoing studies have linked prolonged inflammation caused by low immunity to depression and other mental health issues. As the mental health of young people is increasingly cause for concern, research into the positive effects of beneficial microbes offers hope. One example is the bacterium *Mycobacterium vaccae*, which stimulates the release of seratonin— a natural antidepressant—into the brain.

What are microbes?

These microscopic organisms of single or multiple cells live everywhere, including on and in us. Some make us sick, others are key to our health. Some common types are:

- **Bacteria** These are among the most numerous microbes.
- **Viruses** These infect our cells, cause illness, and damage other microbes.
- **Fungi** Yeasts, mushrooms, and molds are all well-known forms of fungi.
- **Algae** Soil algae are tiny, simple plants, vital for soil fertility.
- **Protozoa** These help decomposition but can cause disease.

The "old friends" theory

One theory suggests that we have evolved with ancient microbes, or "old friends," that we once regularly encountered and that trained our immune systems to fight infections and tolerate harmless allergens. However, due to overuse of antibiotics, eating pasteurized food, and children spending less time playing outdoors, we are no longer exposed to the same range or quantity of microbes.

According to scientists for the British Royal Society for Public Health (RSPH), exposure to "good" bacteria from an early age helps to build a healthy microbiome, as long as "targeted hygiene" is observed, such as washing hands after using the toilet and wearing gloves for gardening if you're not sure what's in your soil or you have scratches or cuts. Many scientific studies show a clear link between childhood exposure to microbes in the soil and food and higher immunity rates as adults, which gives us the perfect excuse to go outside and get digging with the kids.

Regular contact with soil can boost your immune system by increasing your exposure to a variety of beneficial microbes.

The antibiotics beneath our feet

Scientists have found that a significant number of microbes have another important use—as antibiotics. The medical breakthrough penicillin came from *Penicillium*, a fungus found in soil, while the antibiotic vancomycin is made from a bacterium found in dirt. As we become more resistant to the current crop of antibiotics, new research into soil has offered hope—for instance, the development of a new antibiotic, teixobactin, through cultivation of a bacteria called *Eleftheria terrae*. Teixobactin is effective against drug-resistant bacteria such as *Staphylococcus aureus* (MRSA), which is responsible for many human diseases, and *Mycobacterium tuberculosis*, the bacterium that causes tuberculosis.

GET DIGGING TO BOOST IMMUNITY

Encouraging the whole family to get involved in day-to-day gardening jobs, such as weeding or planting, will increase their exposure to beneficial microbes in the soil, potentially boosting their immunity. If you have a garden, why not set aside a section where the children can dig in the dirt? In smaller spaces, they can experiment with growing plants in pots—both indoors and out.

Grow your own

Cultivating your own fruit, vegetables, and herbs can be very rewarding, and getting children on board not only helps them to understand where these foods come from, it may encourage them to eat more fruit and vegetables, too.

Choose crops that grow and fruit quickly (see below), as children can lose interest if plants take too long to produce. Plant fruit and vegetables in a dedicated area or in among flowers. If space is tight, focus on just one or two crops, such as tomatoes or strawberries, which will look great tumbling out of hanging baskets. Indoors, grow herbs on a sunny windowsill and keep plants compact by trimming regularly.

Five easy-to-grow fruits and vegetables

- **Baby carrots** Deliciously sweet and easy to grow
- **Radishes** Super-fast for quick rewards
- **Arugula and baby salad leaves** Tender and quick to crop
- **Dwarf beans or peas** Great for pots and for picking and eating raw
- **Tomatoes and strawberries** Plant varieties for hanging baskets if space is tight

Let your imagination run wild—use colorful containers, such as old boots, to entice your children to grow some fresh edibles in the garden.

Help your wildlife

Be wildlife-friendly while upping your exposure to microbes. Wildflowers are a good pollinator choice, so give them a helping hand—and get your hands really dirty—by molding your own seed bombs. In early spring, scoop up some slightly damp soil or compost, add a little baking flour, and form it into a ball of mucky goodness. Roll it in your wildflower seeds of choice, then let it dry. Throw these seed bombs onto a sunny bed of weed-free soil or onto a lawn, but don't mow the grass. The seeds will soon germinate and flower in summer.

Most kids love digging in the dirt, and some are fascinated by creepy-crawlies too, so why not help them make a wormery? Cut the top and bottom off a large, clear plastic bottle, then plant it in a pot of soil and fill it with layers of damp soil and sand. Add some grass or vegetable peelings on top, then dig up some juicy garden worms to live in their new home. Your kids can watch as the worms pull down the food from above and mix up the layers of soil and sand—soil aeration in action.

Kids will love watching worms in action in a wormery. After a week or so, release your worms and the compost they've made back into the garden.

Cornflowers are easy to grow and will attract butterflies to the garden. Sow seeds in spring for summer flowers.

Five flowers for bees and butterflies

- **Lavender** (*Lavandula*) A bee and butterfly magnet with a relaxing scent.
- **Cornflower** (*Centaurea cyanus*) A wildflower favorite of butterflies as well as bees.
- **Chives** (*Allium schoenoprasum*) Edible leaves and flowers that offer huge nectar rewards for pollinators.
- **Hebe** (*Hebe*) Hardy, long-flowering evergreen shrub with a big nectar hit.
- **Butterfly bush** (*Buddleya*) Butterflies adore the cone-shaped flowers of this easy-to-grow shrub.

Why the garden beats the gym

Research shows that exercising in nature is more beneficial than exercising indoors, and that gardening is one of the best ways to keep fit.

Working in the garden makes us feel good, and research also shows that it helps to keep us fit, increasing muscle strength and bone mineral density, and lowering cholesterol levels, blood pressure, and potentially mortality rates. Recent research offers even more good news: scientists believe that the health benefits of exercising are boosted by being outside in a natural environment.

THE HEALTH BENEFITS OF BEING OUTSIDE

Scientific research shows that exercising in nature, as opposed to working out indoors, stimulates an enzyme called telomerase, which is thought to help regenerate DNA in our chromosomes and potentially prevent age-related illnesses. Stretches of DNA called telomeres form at either end of the chromosomes within a human cell. They prevent damage to the DNA in cells while allowing them to divide without losing any genetic data. Telomere shortening has been linked to aging. To make new blood, bones, skin, and many other parts of the body, cells divide, but each time this process occurs, telomeres get shorter, until eventually cells can no longer divide and become inactive or die.

Our brains are distracted by nature, which means we tend to spend longer working in the garden than we do exercising in the gym.

A study suggests that a person's **lifespan** could potentially be **increased** by **5 years** if their **telomeres** are lengthened

Telomerase is thought to extend the length of telomeres and keep cells healthy, which in turn boosts health and lowers the risk of diseases, such as dementia and cancer. But how does gardening help to increase telomere length? Studies have shown that when exercising outside in nature, our brains are in a more restorative mode (see pp.70–73) and stress levels are lower, which is thought to increase telomerase levels more than when we exercise indoors.

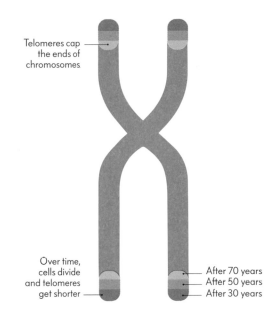

Telomeres cap the ends of chromosomes

Over time, cells divide and telomeres get shorter

After 70 years
After 50 years
After 30 years

TELOMERES SHORTEN AS WE AGE
Chromosomes are found in most living cells and they carry genetic information in the form of genes. As people age, telomeres shorten and eventually cell division stops.

How gardening compares with other forms of exercise

Gardening can be more physically demanding than certain other forms of exercise, such as yoga and gymnastics. It also burns the same amount of calories in 30 minutes as playing badminton, and digging burns as many calories as a fast walk. At the same time, gardening increases muscle strength and flexibility, and exercises joints.

EXERCISING FOR 30 MINUTES

Activity	Calories burned for a 155lb (70kg) person
Running: 5mph (8km/h)	298
Cycling: 12–14mph (19–22km/h)	298
Dancing: fast, ballet, twist	223
Walking: 4.5mph (7km/h)	186
Digging	186
Badminton	167
Gardening: general	167
Gymnastics	149
Stretching, yoga	149

GOOD GARDENING TECHNIQUE

Various different gardening activities, including digging, weeding, planting, and mowing, provide us with an all-body workout. They activate the larger muscle groups, so the heart has to work harder and the body releases hormones that encourage muscle growth and increase metabolism, which burns fat. However, it's important to warm up properly before you start gardening and not work for longer than planned to avoid injury. Poor muscle strength and balance may also contribute to muscle strains and falls.

Building core strength

To prevent injury, build up your core strength and improve your balance with other forms of exercise, such as yoga, Pilates, dancing, or tai chi.

In early spring, after a winter break, limit your gardening time to 90 minutes or less, and then build up the time each week as the season progresses. Remember to warm up before you start: a brisk 10-minute walk will raise your body temperature and warm up your muscles, allowing you to move more freely and making strains less likely. After gardening, perform some simple cooldown stretches, such as calf, thigh, arm, and side stretches, to prevent strains and muscle injury.

Using the right tools is also important in preventing injury—make sure that the shaft of spades and forks is the right length for your height so you don't have to bend over too much. Ask for help if you have to move heavy pots or bags of compost, and switch tasks regularly to avoid repetitive strain injuries.

Good gardening techniques

As well as warming up, cooling down and choosing appropriate tools, specific gardening techniques can also prevent injuries. Research shows that poor posture when digging can almost double the load on the joints, increasing the risk of chronic injuries, especially to the lower back and shoulders. To reduce problems, scientists have devised a method that helps to keep gardeners pain- and injury-free.

Many common garden jobs, such as digging and raking, are great all-around exercises, but a good technique is essential to avoid injury (see right).

Using techniques employed for 3-D animated films, researchers mapped the movement of gardeners while digging and measured the loads imposed on their joints, bones, and muscles. The study showed that good gardening practice involves using a regular, repetitive technique rather than erratic movements. Minimal back bending and large knee bends resulted in fewer injuries, while extended forward bending, limb stretching, and uncontrolled motion caused the most problems.

Mowing the **lawn** for **30 minutes** with a **push mower** burns as many **calories** as **golf** or **ballroom dancing**

Keep your neck and shoulders relaxed to reduce strain

GOOD TECHNIQUE

Avoid back pain and joint injury by paying attention to your posture and alignment when digging, lifting, weeding, and carrying in the garden.

Keep your back straight and bend at the knee to take the load off your spine

Avoid twisting your knees and align your kneecaps with your toes when bending or kneeling

The Nourishing Garden

Introduction

Maintain your soil's health and your green space will flourish, producing a bounty of nutrient-rich fruit and vegetables, together with health-boosting medicinal plants.

Good soil is so much more than "dirt" to gardeners. Well-nourished earth is alive with microbes, fungi, insects, worms, and other organisms, all of which produce the nutrients required to keep plants—and, ultimately, us—healthy. You can boost your garden's fertility in a number of sustainable ways, and once your soil is nourished, you'll be ready to plant your edibles. Growing your own food is one of the most satisfying aspects of gardening, particularly when your harvest arrives at your table bursting with vitamins, minerals, and flavor. If your soil is contaminated, there are other ways to grow edibles safely, and it's easy to produce a range of crops even in a small garden or on a patio or balcony. Your green space can be a natural medicine chest, too. Most medicines were once derived from plants, and many new ones still are. Your garden, balcony, or windowsill could become your source of natural, plant-based remedies to treat a range of ailments.

The secret life of healthy soil

Good soil is the key to keeping plants healthy, and an army of organisms helps to keep it in good condition.

Soil is full of life: a quarter of all known species live in it, recycling material and making nutrients available for plants. Healthy soil consists of millions of these tiny organisms, along with air, water, organic matter, and mineral particles. Soil health matters to us all—healthy soil is essential to our global food supplies, among other things—but there is a rapidly growing problem of soil erosion and degradation. A 2006 study warned that global soil is being washed away 10 to 40 times faster than it's being replaced.

FUNGI AS NATURAL FERTILIZER

Plants need nutrients, including nitrogen, potassium, and phosphorous, for strong, healthy growth. Usually, they get these nutrients from air, water, and soil. However, when soil becomes degraded, lacking sufficient air and organic matter, it can no longer hold moisture and provide the right environment for soil organisms. This can lead to soil erosion as plants fail to thrive. While fertilizers can increase nutrient levels, high concentrations of aritifical fertlizers can inhibit natural soil organisms, especially fungi, which are key to good soil. The smarter, more sustainable option is to keep soil healthy so that plants can obtain nutrients naturally.

A network of nutrients

One of the most important soil organisms for plants is fungi. Mycorrhizal fungi form symbiotic relationships with plant roots. They help plants to absorb water, access less readily available nutrients such as phosphorous, and fight off harmful predators in the soil. In exchange, fungi get food as carbohydrates from the host.

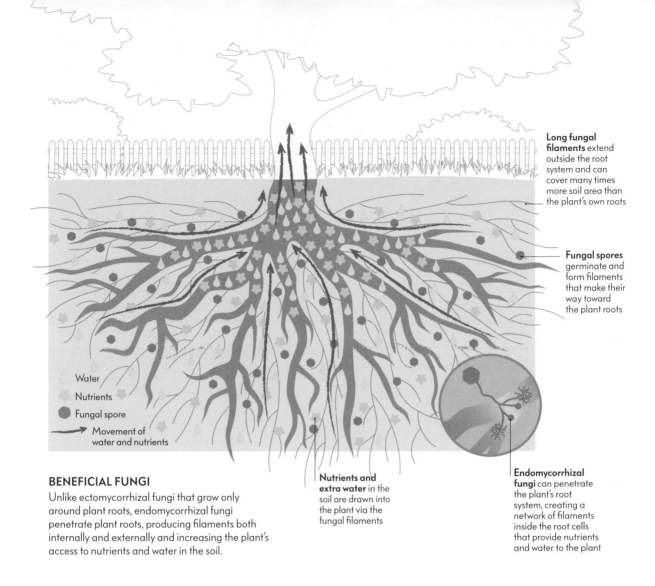

Long fungal filaments extend outside the root system and can cover many times more soil area than the plant's own roots

Fungal spores germinate and form filaments that make their way toward the plant roots

Water

Nutrients

Fungal spore

→ Movement of water and nutrients

BENEFICIAL FUNGI

Unlike ectomycorrhizal fungi that grow only around plant roots, endomycorrhizal fungi penetrate plant roots, producing filaments both internally and externally and increasing the plant's access to nutrients and water in the soil.

Nutrients and extra water in the soil are drawn into the plant via the fungal filaments

Endomycorrhizal fungi can penetrate the plant's root system, creating a network of filaments inside the root cells that provide nutrients and water to the plant

Mycorrhizal fungi form intricate networks of hairlike filaments in and around the roots of plants, and between plants, to make a flourishing soil ecosystem that maintains soil structure and protects against erosion. Ectomycorrhizal fungi grow only around the roots of plants, but the majority are endomycorrhizal, which penetrate the roots. Scientists have discovered that these fungal networks can also connect nearby plants of the same species, enabling them to share resources and even signal to each other to warn of pest attacks.

You can add these beneficial fungi to your soil (see p.136) to help your plants absorb water and nutrients more easily. To improve your soil's structure and fertility, add organic matter (such as a mulch and well-rotted garden compost) to boost your earthworm population, and use techniques such as no-dig cultivation (see p.136).

At least **80 percent** of all land **plant species** are known to form **mycorrhizal** fungal networks

BOOSTING YOUR SOIL

There are simple ways to check the state of your own soil. Healthy soil that is left undisturbed will develop a honeycomblike structure of tiny air passages due to the work of numerous soil organisms, allowing air and moisture to infiltrate. If your beds have a healthy population of earthworms, which only thrive in moist soils rich in organic matter, and if your plants are growing strongly with lots of foliage and flowers, then your soil is likely to be in excellent condition. However, yellowing or discolored leaves, poor flowering, and stunted growth may be signs of degrading soil, in which case there are steps you can take to help it recover.

The no-dig method

The good news is there's very little work involved. Traditionally, gardeners regularly dig organic material, such as compost, into the soil to improve it. But this disturbs the structures that soil organisms make. The no-dig method aims to protect these structures and maintain carbon levels in the soil that digging potentially depletes.

Cover your beds with a generous layer of peat-free biodegradable mulch (see opposite), such as garden or green-waste compost, or well-rotted manure. The organic matter will gradually be broken down by soil organisms, including worms. Digging delivers oxygen to dormant weed seeds, so by leaving soil undisturbed, these fail to grow. Meanwhile, the mulch layer blocks the light to weeds, causing them to die off. If any weeds germinate from windblown seeds, pull them out by hand. This approach saves time on weeding and watering, and consistently results in higher yields. In trials with vegetables grown side by side in "dig" and "no-dig" beds, the "no-dig" beds regularly produced a more generous harvest. A good layer of mulch also protects the soil, especially in winter when heavy rain can pound upper layers.

Digging-in methods

If you have poor soil—if your house is a new-build without an established garden, for instance—you may need to initially dig in organic matter to increase your soil's capacity to hold water and nutrients. Half a wheelbarrow of organic matter per 11sq ft (square meter) will give plants a great head start.

You can buy mycorrhizal fungi in powder form and lightly dust it over the roots of herbaceous plants, shrubs, and trees when planting. Organic fertilizers, such as seaweed, fish blood and bone, bonemeal, or liquid comfrey can also help provide many nutrients.

Healthy soil produces plants that are more resilient and can cope better with disease and drought. Nourishing your soil helps it to remain productive.

WHAT KIND OF MULCH?

Biodegradable mulches help retain moisture and slowly break down to release nutrients in the soil, providing food for soil organisms and plants. You can make your own compost and leaf mold, or buy it ready-made.

1 Garden waste breaks down quickly into compost and is a good source of nitrogen (see pp.204–205).

2 Well-rotted wood chippings form a carbon-rich and long-lasting mulch.

3 Animal manure provides a rich mulch where vegetables will flourish, but make sure it is well rotted, otherwise it can scorch young plants.

4 Spent mushroom compost is good for acid soils as it can increase soil alkalinity, or you can alternate it with other mulches.

5 Leaf mold is an effective soil conditioner and you can use it when it has fully rotted down with other composts to make compost for seed-sowing.

Let earthworms do the work

Earthworms are described as "ecosystem engineers:" they digest organic matter, releasing it back into the soil, and their tunnels allow roots to spread and access air, water, and nutrients. A recent study of crop yields found that earthworms stimulate growth by up to 25 percent. Scientists suggest this is because they release nitrogen locked away in the soil. You can make your garden earthworm friendly or buy earthworms online to add to planting beds, but be sure you provide enough organic matter (either dug in or as mulch) for them to survive.

The detoxing power of plants

Soil contamination can be harmful to health, so if you're growing edibles, it's important to have pollutant-free soil.

Could your soil contain pollutants? Like other forms of pollution, soil contamination is a worldwide problem. Once again, plants can come to the rescue, taking up harmful toxins from contaminated soil across large areas. However, this purifying process can take years, so if you are growing edibles, a quicker, more practical way to be sure that you're growing them safely is to replace topsoil or use raised beds filled with new soil.

TOXIC SOIL AND ITS HARMFUL EFFECTS

If you're growing flowers in the garden, then contaminated soil is not really a problem, but if you're growing edibles, it's wise to make sure your soil is clean.

Soil contamination is typically caused by wastes from mining and manufacturing, vehicle emissions, agricultural poisons, and chemical and sewage leaks. Bonfires, heating systems, and fossil-fuel combustion also contribute. The main groups of contaminants in soil include heavy metals, persistent organic pollutants (POPs)—caused by vehicle emissions and burning fossil fuels—and radioactive contaminants.

A 2013 study found that concentrations of soil contaminants in plant foods, or in the soil we breathe in or touch, can cause a range of health problems, including cancers, neurological damage and low IQ, reproductive disorders, kidney disease, skeletal and bone diseases, and an increase in birth defects.

Rise above the problem

If you want to grow fruit and vegetables, test your soil *before* you start growing. You can use a soil-testing kit for toxic materials or have your soil professionally tested. If the results show that

HOW PLANTS PROCESS TOXINS

Plants can store toxins in their tissues, taking them out of circulation. They can also reduce the impact of toxins by stabilizing them or breaking them down.

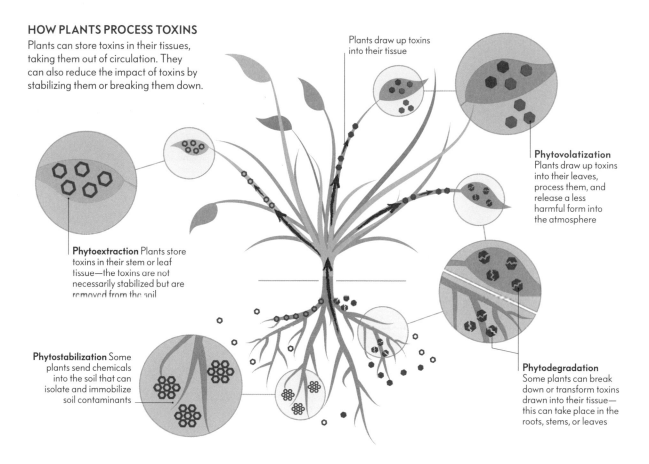

Plants draw up toxins into their tissue

Phytovolatization
Plants draw up toxins into their leaves, process them, and release a less harmful form into the atmosphere

Phytoextraction Plants store toxins in their stem or leaf tissue—the toxins are not necessarily stabilized but are removed from the soil

Phytostabilization Some plants send chemicals into the soil that can isolate and immobilize soil contaminants

Phytodegradation Some plants can break down or transform toxins drawn into their tissue—this can take place in the roots, stems, or leaves

your soil is contaminated, one solution is to replace it with clean topsoil to a depth suitable for the vegetables you want to grow. You can also use a geotextile membrane to lay over the surface of contaminated soils to separate them from clean soils—although be aware that water, which can carry contaminants, will still be able to move between the two.

Alternatively, an excellent way to make sure your fruit and vegetables are not contaminated is to grow them in raised beds, containers, or hanging baskets with compost or good-quality soil, rather than growing directly in the ground.

Plants that detox the soil

Certain plants are particularly good at drawing up toxins from the soil while resisting their harmful effects themselves. After the nuclear accident in 1986 in Chernobyl, in what is now Ukraine, sunflowers were used in the 1990s to clean radioactive soil and groundwater, and they were used again in Fukushima, Japan, after the nuclear accident there in 2011. Elsewhere, broad-leaved trees, such as willows, are helping to clear heavy metals from mining and landfill sites. A Finnish study showed some willows may bring zinc in soil down to acceptable levels in just 6 years, nickel in 10, and copper in 15 to 50. Instead of dumping polluted soil in landfills, plants could potentially provide a cheaper, less invasive way of cleaning large contaminated areas.

DESIGNING YOUR PERFECT RAISED BED

Growing edibles in raised beds is a good solution to soil contamination, and they offer several other advantages. Elevating the soil can improve the drainage and create ideal growing conditions. The soil in raised beds warms up earlier and stays warm later in the season, resulting in a longer growing period. It's easy to control weeds in a confined space, and for gardeners with mobility problems, taller raised beds are more accessible. A raised bed can also be an opportunity to express your garden's particular style.

When siting your raised bed, consider the proportions of your garden, as well as its aspect in relation to the sun, to determine the best shape and location for it. If you only have space for a small bed, you may prefer to put it close to the house for easy access. Allow plenty of space to move around the bed and make sure you can easily reach the middle. Installing raised beds of different heights creates interest and structure in the garden, and allows for different crops. Group them together or lay them in a grid pattern for a sense of geometry.

Material thoughts

There is a huge selection of materials to suit all styles and budgets, from the rustic appearance of wattle to stone and terracotta, and galvanized or rusted metal. Lumber boards, bricks, or concrete blocks are long-lasting and sturdy.

Dividers in your beds allow you to have a variety of soil types and conditions in each section, so you can grow moisture-loving basil beside drought-tolerant thyme, for instance.

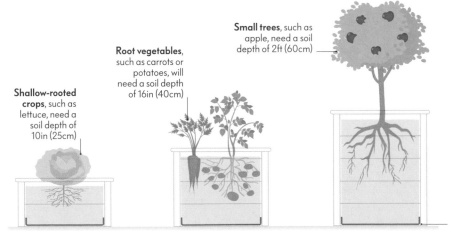

Shallow-rooted crops, such as lettuce, need a soil depth of 10in (25cm)

Root vegetables, such as carrots or potatoes, will need a soil depth of 16in (40cm)

Small trees, such as apple, need a soil depth of 2ft (60cm)

HOW DEEP TO BUILD

The ideal depth for a raised bed depends on your crops: a shallow bed is fine for salad greens, but you'll need more than twice that to allow for the deep roots of a fruit tree. The width should not exceed 5ft (1.5m) so you can access plants from both sides. Raised beds on hard surfaces drain better with a depth of about 2ft (60cm).

Lining the base of the bed ensures that roots don't grow through into the contaminated soil

Wood is a relatively cheap and versatile option for raised beds—you can adapt it for a variety of effects, such as rustic, natural, or colorful.

Metal beds are an economical option that will suit a more contemporary garden.

Try experimenting with a mix of materials and shapes for your raised beds to add visual interest.

Beds of different heights allow you to compartmentalize crops and grow ones that need varying soil depths.

A KITCHEN GARDEN
This abundantly productive kitchen garden is also a beautifully designed space. Herbs such as lavender and rosemary introduce Mediterranean aromas along the main path. Design by Matt Keightley.

A medicine chest in the garden

Plants have long been used to treat ailments and are the source of many of our modern medicines.

Flowers and other plant parts can help to treat a myriad of diseases and disorders, from burns and poor digestion to cancers, heart disease, and even Alzheimer's. Modern medicine uses more than 35,500 different plants for treatments, and scientists believe that many more plant-based cures are yet to be discovered. You can grow your own medicinal plants in your green space to treat a number of conditions, and, with many plants facing extinction, growing a broad range of species could also help to conserve precious medicines for the future.

POWERFUL PLANT CURES

Throughout history and in all cultures, people have used plants to treat health conditions. All plants produce chemical compounds, or phytochemicals, and humans have known about the curative powers of certain phytochemicals for millennia. Ancient texts mention willow as a treatment for fever and pain, for instance. Willow's active ingredient, salicin, was a precursor of aspirin, one of the most commonly used pain-relievers. Scientists are discovering new medicinal uses for plants all the time—chemicals in yew, for example, have cancer-fighting properties and have been used to make chemotherapy drugs since the 1990s.

Today, about 40 percent of our prescription medicines come from plant extracts or synthesized plant compounds, and we've tapped only a tiny fraction of our fast-disappearing botanical riches. Set aside part of your green space to be a medicine chest of plant remedies. Not all conditions can be treated with home-grown remedies, but some plant-based treatments have a good track record for managing many minor ailments (see pp.146–149).

FOXGLOVE
(*Digitalis lanata*)
Foxglove contains the chemical **digoxin**, which is effective in the treatment of **heart disease,** although the same chemical makes foxgloves **potentially fatal** if ingested.

YEW
(*Taxus baccata*)
The **needles** of both the **English yew tree** and the **Pacific yew tree** are used in the **chemotherapy** drug **taxol**.

FEVERFEW
(*Tanacetum parthenium*)
This herb is traditionally used to treat **migraines**. **Research** in **France** and **Germany** supports its **efficacy**, but scientists are unsure **how** it works.

VALERIAN
(*Valeriana officinalis*)
Valerian reduces **stress** and is used as a **sleep** aid. Scientists believe that **phytochemicals** in the plant's **essential oil** are responsible for the **sedative** effects.

DAFFODILS
(*Narcissus*)
Galantamine, found in **daffodils**, is used to treat mild to moderate **Alzheimer's disease.** It helps to regulate a brain messenger that plays a role in **learning** and **memory**.

POPPIES
(*Papaver somniferum*)
The **oldest** written evidence of medicinal plants' usage mentions **poppies**. A chemical in the **opium poppy's** seedpod is the main active ingredient in **morphine** and **codeine**, the **world's** most widely used **analgesics**.

WARNING
Most parts of **yew** are toxic, and the foliage in particular can be fatal if eaten. All parts of **foxglove** can result in severe poisoning if eaten. **Daffodils** are also toxic if eaten but not life-threatening.

DESIGNING A MEDICINAL GARDEN

Before you start planting (see pp.148–149), consider the design of your medicinal garden. If you have space, you can create a dedicated herb garden, or weave a selection of your favorites into an existing ornamental border or vegetable garden. Herbs in hanging baskets or containers on a roof terrace or balcony, or in a window box, will also provide a good crop.

Making space

If you have space for a dedicated herb garden, situate it near your kitchen so you can pick the herbs as and when you need them. Decide whether you want a formal layout, such as a grid of beds, or a more informal design with herbs planted in drifts. Divide beds with permeable paths of gravel or wooden walkways, or interplant paving slabs with low-growing herbs, such as creeping thyme or chamomile, which release their fragrance where you walk (see also p.94).

A small, decorative chamomile lawn can be an attractive feature for your medicinal garden. Chamomile will tolerate only very light foot traffic, but you can harvest the daisylike flowers for teas when they bloom in summer.

If you have heavy clay soil, raised beds (see pp.140–141) are a good option for many medicinal herbs because they offer the free drainage many of these plants require. When planting directly in the ground, add a few bucketfuls of horticultural grit to clay-rich soils to aid drainage.

Room to grow

Check the final heights and spreads of the plants you plan to grow and give them space to expand. Annual medicinal plants, such as calendulas, can be interspersed among other garden plants, but perennials need a location for the longer term. Put taller plants in the center of a raised bed or at the back of a border, so that they don't shade smaller plants in front—most herbs need full sun. A young rosemary plant, for example, may develop into a 3ft (1m) tall bush after a few years. If space is limited, some plants, such as bay, rosemary, and lavender, can be trained as standards.

Group your plants according to their requirements, such as whether they prefer full sun or can tolerate partial shade. Pocket planters attached to a wall or fence, or fabric saddle baskets hooked on railings, are good space-saving ideas for small gardens and balconies, and allow easy access to the herbs for regular harvesting to make teas and infusions.

Stack your pots on a ladder to create a tower of herbs in the corner of a patio or on a balcony.

Formal herb gardens, such as this one, feature square or rectangular beds in a neat, symmetrical layout.

If space in the garden is tight, you can grow herbs in pocket planters attached to a wall. Consider irrigation and watering needs when you set it up.

Even if you don't have a garden or balcony, many herbs will thrive on a sunny windowsill.

GROW YOUR
OWN REMEDIES

By growing your own medicinal plants, you can experiment with different ways of drying and storing them. First, make a list of the medicinal plants you want to use and what kind of conditions they prefer, such as damp and shady or sunny and free-draining. Group plants with similar requirements together.

If you have space, grow a selection of shrubs, perennials, annuals, and trees. In smaller gardens, choose more compact herbs, such as chamomile, sage, fleabane, and calendulas.

Some herbs, including peppermint, lemon balm, and woodruff, will spread rapidly through the garden if left unchecked. Grow them in large pots where space is limited or to prevent them from swamping other plants. Unlike the majority of herbs, these plants are also happy in low-light conditions and will thrive on a shady balcony.

You can also grow tender, sun-loving plants such as chilli peppers and aloe vera in containers outside after all risk of frost has passed. Bring them inside when the weather turns cold again, but be sure they still have plenty of sunlight. Aloe vera also makes an attractive houseplant.

Medicinal uses

You can use medicinal plants in several ways to treat common ailments or as a pick-me-up (see opposite). One of the easiest ways to enjoy the benefits is to brew herbal teas and infusions, but you can also use your plants to make ointments and creams. Use leaves or flowers for teas—they will grow back quickly when you pick them during the growing season, but avoid harvesting in winter, when most plants are dormant.

Summer teas from fresh leaves, such as mint or lemon verbena, are an easy starting point, and if you have an abundant harvest, you can dry and store herb leaves for a year-round supply. Spread out the leaves in a warm, dark, well-ventilated area to dry, turning them over several times during the first few days so that air reaches every surface. When they are completely free of moisture and crumble easily, store the leaves in a dark glass jar with an air-tight lid. They will keep for about a year.

Other remedies make use of plant roots or stems. There are plenty of recipes online or in print for plant-based medicinal remedies, but use a trusted source. Experiment with more complex preparations as your skills develop, but always seek medical advice before using any plant-based remedies.

PLANT REMEDIES

These healing plants are easy to grow, and can be made into teas and infusions, or balms and lotions.

PLANTS FOR TEAS AND INFUSIONS

1 Chamomile (*Chamaemelum nobile, Matricaria recutita*) Use the white daisylike flowers of this low-growing perennial fresh or dried to make a tea to help reduce stress and induce sleep.

2 Lemon balm (*Melissa officinalis*) Teas made with this calming perennial herb help to relieve anxiety and stress, and overcome insomnia.

Other options

- **Angelica** (*Angelica archangelica*) The roots of this tall, architectural perennial help to relieve menstrual cramps and aid digestion.
- **Mexican fleabane** (*Erigeron karvinskianus*) Use the leaves and the white and pink daisy flowers of this little perennial plant to alleviate kidney disorders and menstrual pain.
- **Woodruff** (*Galium odoratum*) This evergreen perennial's flowers and leaves help to relieve anxiety and induce sleep, and can also reduce the symptoms of arthritis.
- **Peppermint** (*Mentha* x *piperita*) An age-old remedy for stomachaches, this leafy perennial herb aids digestion and reduces the symptoms of irritable bowel syndrome (IBS).
- **Rosemary** (*Rosmarinus officinalis*) Known as the "herb of remembrance" in folklore, this evergreen shrub's leaves help to improve memory and concentration (see p.93).
- **Sage** (*Salvia officinalis*) The leaves of this evergreen shrub help to relieve the symptoms of menopause, such as hot flashes, and may also aid digestion.

PLANTS FOR BALMS AND LOTIONS

3 Calendula (*Calendula officinalis*) The flowers of this versatile annual have both antiseptic and anti-inflammatory properties.

4 Witch hazel (*Hamamelis virginiana*) The roots have astringent and antiviral properties that soothe sprains and help to tighten skin pores and treat acne.

Other options

- **Lavender** (*Lavandula*) The flowers of this small shrub help to soothe frayed nerves and promote sleep.
- **Aloe vera** (*Aloe vera*) The gel in the fleshy leaves has anti-inflammatory and antibacterial properties, as well as a hormone that repairs skin damage.

Growing your own food

For a nutrient-rich diet full of flavor, consider devoting some space to growing your own fruit and vegetables.

A diet rich in fresh fruit and vegetables is vital to our health, providing vitamins, minerals, and other nutrients that perform hundreds of essential roles in the body, as well as reducing the risk of heart disease, cancer, and many other illnesses. However, in many cases crops lose nutritional value during their journey from farm to fork. By growing your own produce, you can restore these key nutrients to your diet—choose vitamin-rich and flavorful varieties that often aren't readily available in supermarkets.

VANISHING NUTRIENTS IN FOOD

Fruit and vegetables contain vitamins, macronutrients such as nitrogen and phosphorus, and micronutrients such as calcium and zinc, that people need to thrive. Many vegetables also contain antioxidants, which help to prevent oxygen reacting with other chemicals, a process that is thought to damage our DNA and may be linked to aging and degenerative diseases.

Today, commercial crops contain measurably fewer nutrients than they used to. Over many decades, the large-scale production of certain crops, the time taken to transport them from harvest to plate, and storage practices—such as

Green vegetables in the **cabbage family** (broccoli, kale, Savoy cabbage, and Brussels sprouts) contain potential **cancer-fighting** chemicals called **glucosinolates**. The British **broccoli variety 'Beneforte'** has been bred to produce **three times** more glucosinolate than usual.

Pale vegetables such as **onions** and **garlic** contain **antioxidant** and **anti-inflammatory** compounds that may be useful in preventing **degenerative diseases**. **Mushrooms** can be an excellent source of **Vitamin D**, essential for **healthy bones** and **teeth**.

Purple plant-based foods contain **polyphenols** that are thought to help to lower the risk of many **diseases**, including **cancer**.

Red chilli peppers contain **capsanthin**, a **carotenoid** that may have **cancer-fighting** properties. **Tomatoes** contain **lycopene**, a **polyphenol** linked to a reduced risk of **prostate cancer**.

lengthy refrigeration—can strip valuable nutrients from our food. A UK study that measured nutrients in 20 vegetables between 1930 and 1980, for instance, found that iron levels had fallen by 22 percent, calcium levels by 19 percent, and potassium by 14 percent. This means that, in some cases, you would need to eat many times more of a fruit or vegetable—eight times as many in the case of oranges, for instance—to get the same amount of nutrients as people did two generations ago. The good news is that, by selecting high-nutrient plant varieties and growing your own, you can boost your diet with nutrient-rich fruit and vegetables.

In addition to vitamins and minerals, your healthy crop will contain chemicals called phytonutrients, such as carotenoids (plant pigments) and polyphenols. Although they are not vital for our immediate survival, phytonutrients are still beneficial for our health, and research shows that they can potentially help to prevent diseases, such as cancer. Many phytonutrients give plants their pigments, so include a range of colors in your diet for a variety of phytonutrients.

Maximizing nutrients

How you harvest, store, and cook your fruit and vegetables also has an effect on their nutritional value. Fresh is often best when it comes to many green leafy vegetables, and growing your own puts them on your plate in seconds. The levels of health-giving chemicals in some fruits and vegetables, such as tomatoes and winter squashes, actually increase when they are stored at room temperature after harvesting.

Microwaving, sautéing, or steaming are, in many cases, often better at preserving nutrients than boiling, as soluble nutrients will leach into the water. A UK study in 2012 found that cooking in water not only decreased broccoli's nutrients, but also that purple-sprouting broccoli, which contains more nutrients than green broccoli, lost significantly more nutrient value after boiling than the green variety.

Orange and **yellow fruits** and **vegetables** contain **carotenes**, believed to have a number of **health benefits**, including protecting **eye health**. They may also lower the risk of some **cancers**.

PREPARE FOR PLANTING

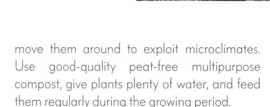

No matter what size your green space, there's always room to grow your own produce. Choose your favorite nutrient-rich varieties, give them the conditions they need to flourish, and you'll reap healthy and flavorful crops. First, though, you need to prepare for planting to give yourself the best chance of a rewarding harvest.

Planting in the ground

The starting point for healthy produce is a rich, living soil, teeming with soil organisms (see pp.134–137). Plants growing in healthy soil are more resilient and will cope better with adverse weather conditions such as flooding and drought. Mulch your soil regularly (see p.137) to add nutrients and help to retain moisture.

Depending on space, decide whether you want to dedicate an area to vegetables or grow them with perennials and other flowering plants. Mixing the vegetables into a border can showcase attractive vegetable varieties. Either way, choose a sheltered spot away from strong winds. Avoid planting the same vegetables in the same place in consecutive years to prevent the buildup of pests and diseases in the soil.

Containerized growing

Many fruits and vegetables are happy growing in containers as long as they have good drainage. Containers offer many advantages over growing in the ground: they are perfect for small spaces—a windowbox of herbs will give a good crop of leaves for cooking and herbal teas for months (see pp.148–149)—and you can move them around to exploit microclimates. Use good-quality peat-free multipurpose compost, give plants plenty of water, and feed them regularly during the growing period.

If you have space, raised beds (see pp.140–141) are a good option for your kitchen garden, particularly if the soil in your garden is poor quality or contaminated (see pp.138–139).

Sowing seeds

Starting vegetables from seed is the most economical way to get plenty of plants. Transplant the seedlings once they are large enough to handle. Plant young tomato, chilli, and bell pepper plants in peat-free multipurpose compost, but keep them indoors until the risk of frost has passed. Harden the plants off by placing them outside during the day before transplanting outside in a final position, a peat-free grow-bag, or container.

Brassicas, onions, leeks, and lettuce prefer to be started in seed trays indoors or a sheltered place outdoors, before planting. Some vegetables prefer to be sown directly in situ, particularly root vegetables such as carrots, beets, beans, parsnips, peas, and radishes. With a little planning, your kitchen garden can be productive all year round (see pp.154–155).

Although you can sow vegetable seeds all year, apart from December and January, most vegetables are sown early in spring. Sow root vegetables such as carrots and parsnips outdoors directly in their final positions.

If you have poor quality soil, add some well-rotted garden compost before you start planting to help seedlings thrive.

One serving (about 4oz /120g) of **fruit** or **vegetables** may have as many as **100** different types of **phytonutrients**

Beets are easy to grow and you can sow seed outside from mid-April to July. The young leaves make a tasty and nutritious addition to salads.

A YEAR OF VEGETABLES

Growing your own greens allows you to put fresh, delicious vegetables on your plate in seconds, which is key to preserving the nutrients in the leaves of many crops. With careful planning, you can harvest healthy greens all year round, even in a small space.

Successional sowing

To avoid having a glut of vegetables ready to harvest at the same time, sow in batches so that they mature in succession, giving a steadier supply. Try batch planting with carrots, radishes, kohlrabi, beets, and spinach, sowing every two or three weeks in the growing season, or, as leaves appear from one batch, sow the next.

Some salad greens are ready in a short time and are useful to keep as ongoing crops. Sow batches of seed in containers or on a windowsill every four to six weeks for a continuous supply. You can either harvest the leaves when young by snipping them off when they reach about 6in (15cm) in height, leaving the stubs to regrow for a second crop, or thin the seedlings if you want larger, mature heads to develop. Try endives, cutting lettuces, mustard, arugula, spinach, and Swiss chard.

Radish and mustard seedlings can be ready in as little as eight weeks, and you can pick a few leaves for salads and stir fries before then. Other greens take slightly longer, such as beets,

fennel, summer lettuces, spring onions, and early peas. If you are growing cabbages to harvest the head, make a cross-shaped score with a knife on the stem after harvesting the head—it will resprout to provide more leaves.

Filling the "hungry gap"

A combination of fast-maturing salad leaves and hardy overwintering vegetables can provide fresh produce in the "hungry gap" in late winter and through the spring. For a fall crop, sow hardy vegetables such as purple-sprouting broccoli in trays in a greenhouse or on a windowsill and plant out in mid-spring a few weeks before the last frosts. For a late winter/early spring crop, sow seeds in situ from late spring to midsummer. Other hardy vegetables include winter and spring cabbages, leeks, hardy mustards, kale, and winter lettuces.

Hardy salads include oriental leaves such as mizuna, mustard, and arugula, as well as corn salad and chard. The salads will need protection outside, such as a horticultural fleece or a cloche, in the coldest conditions. Nasturtiums and violas are hardy plants that you can sow in early spring, or late summer if you want winter- to early spring-flowering violas. The flowers and leaves make a tasty accompaniment to salads.

Indoor sprouting

Where space is at a premium, sprout some seeds indoors to sprinkle on salads or use in stir fries. Buy untreated seeds that are sold for sprouting and put them in a jar after soaking. Seeds ideal for sprouting include mung beans, cress, alfalfa, and adzuki beans.

Butterhead lettuce (top left) matures quickly and tolerates poorer growing conditions. Pick the young leaves of kale 'Red Russian' and mizuna (top right) to add to salads. Alfalfa sprouts (above) are easy to grow and can provide a year-round crop, while you can harvest the stems and leaves of Swiss chard 'Bright Lights' (left) about 10 weeks after sowing.

MAKING SMALL SPACES FRUITFUL

Size doesn't matter—even the smallest space can produce a crop of fruit. Most fruit plants need full sun or at least some sun, and dislike wind and frost, so choose a sheltered, sunny spot on your balcony or in your garden. In temperate areas, even tender fruit plants such as figs will grow if you protect them from frost—take plants in containers inside, and protect a fan-trained plant with bracken or straw and then cover with horticultural fleece.

For the smallest areas, grow fruiting plants such as strawberries in a terracotta pot, hanging basket, or windowbox. Snip off or repot runners to keep the plants contained. As with any plants in containers, you'll need to be vigilant about regular feeding and watering.

Dwarf types

Grow your own apples, cherries, and plums for a crop of delicious fruits and trees that add color and structure to the garden. Some red-skinned apples, such as 'Braeburn', 'Red Delicious', 'Red Falstaff', and 'Pink Lady' contain the highest concentrations of polyphenols. 'Red Love' can contain up to twice the polyphenols of a regular apple. A number of fruit trees are available on dwarfing rootstock, which will keep the size in check while also producing a good crop of fruit.

Many fruit trees need cross-pollination—a different cultivar of the same fruit needs to pollinate their flowers. Check which other trees need to be near for your fruit trees to crop well.

Vertical spaces

To make good use of your space, you can train apple and pear trees as cordons, fans, and espaliers to grow on walls and fences or on either side of an arch. Cordons will work well in the ground or in containers. You can buy trees pretrained to the desired shape. Maintain the shape of the plant as it grows with sturdy supporting wires on a wall or fence. Redcurrants and gooseberries can also be grown as cordons with one vertical stem that produces spurs of fruit, and these plants will tolerate some shade.

You can also buy or train apple trees as step-over plants—low-growing, horizontally trained trees about 18in (45cm) high. They look great bordering the edge of a path but, as for all trained trees, need careful pruning in summer and winter to remain in shape.

Planting and aftercare

When planting, add some mycorrhizal fungi (see p.135) to the bottom of the hole, close to the root ball, and add some mulch on top to help to retain moisture. Water your fruit trees well during dry or windy spells for the first two years after planting while they are getting established.

Make a feature of your apple tree—and save space, too—by training it as an espalier on a sheltered, sunny wall or fence.

Strawberries are easy to grow in containers, provided they have sun and are sheltered from wind and frost. The perpetual varieties will produce fruit from early summer to early fall.

Growing fruit such as pears in cordons allows you to grow several cultivars in a small space and create a striking fruiting screen.

Gooseberry plants can be trained to grow as standards to make good use of vertical space in a small garden.

157

AN ABUNDANT GARDEN

In this large chef's kitchen garden, I was able to devote one type of vegetable to each raised bed—here you can see ruby chard—and I then filled the boundary borders with ornamental flowers to create a riot of color. To the left, the delicate flowers of fennel have self-seeded along the paths. Design by Matt Keightley.

The
Sustainable
Garden

Introduction

Turn your garden into an environmentally friendly space that provides shade, insulation, and protection against drought and flood, while offering a haven for pollinators, too.

Temperatures are predicted to rise as global warming and a changing climate take hold, but a single shade tree or a climber can take some of the heat off your home. Trees and wall shrubs shield buildings from wind, rain, and snow, and evergreen climbers provide an insulating buffer. Water shortages are set to become more common, but selecting drought-resistant plants, including some tree species, drastically reduces the amount of water needed to maintain them. If your area is prone to flooding, choose porous surfaces, such as lawns, instead of impermeable paving, and select plants that store water to help prevent flooding and soil erosion. Using plants that suit your environment and composting waste are keys to keeping your garden "green" in a truly sustainable sense. Many plants are lifesavers for pollinating insects, such as bees. Create a home for them by providing nectar-rich flowers, reducing pesticide use, and making wild areas, such as wildflower meadows, part of your garden. By planting a cut-flower garden for indoor arrangements, instead of using imported blooms, you'll reduce your carbon footprint and help pollinators, too.

The cooling effect of plants

When summer temperatures soar, shade-giving trees, climbers, and planted rooftops can help to cool us down.

Hard surfaces, such as buildings, pavements, and roads, absorb almost all the heat from the sun and radiate it back into the atmosphere at night. Called the "heat island effect," this raises air temperature. Plants, however, can help cool our homes and cities by using some of this solar energy to transport water from roots to leaves, and by absorption, reflection, and shading.

Solar radiation

Dense canopies with a high leaf-area index and thick leaves are effective at cooling the ground and other surfaces

When shaded by trees, buildings and other hard surfaces absorb and store less heat, releasing less back into the atmosphere

Up to 90 percent of solar radiation is blocked by the canopy

A TREE TO KEEP COOL
Trees act like giant parasols by directly blocking the sun's rays, keeping the soil and surrounding buildings cooler.

People in the shade of the tree radiate some of their body heat to the cooler ground. This can reduce the temperature they feel their surroundings to be by between 13° and 27°F (7° and 15°C)

The ground can be about 22°F (12°C) cooler in the shade of a tree

SOAKING UP THE SUN

According to predictions about the effects of a changing climate, there will be more intense and more frequent summer heatwaves in the future. Heatwaves aren't just uncomfortable or life-threatening for the vulnerable—electricity demand soars as we turn on air-conditioning units and electric fans, increasing the creation of polluting carbon emissions.

Keep cool with plants

Trees and other plants can help. Studies show that a tree can block up to 90 percent of the sun's radiation with its canopy and by diverting some of it to transpiration (the process of transporting water from the roots to the leaves to be released as water vapor). The shade cast by a tree can cover an area up to 50 percent larger than its canopy. In one study of street trees in the UK, this shady ground was shown to be on average 22°F (12°C) cooler than ground in the sun.

Buildings also benefit from shade cast by trees—trees with a denser canopy have more of a cooling effect. Experimental research in the US shows that the shade from trees can cut the costs of air-conditioning in detached houses by up to 30 percent.

Sheltering green roofs and walls

Plants on roofs cool the surface by shading, absorbing, and reflecting incoming solar energy, and by transpiration. Indoor temperatures are shown to be 5°–7°F (3°-4°C) lower below a green roof when the outside temperature is between 59° and 86°F (15° and 30°C).

Covering outside walls with climbers or installing a living wall (see p.170) can also keep buildings cool. Research shows that an evergreen climber such as ivy cools façades mainly by shading, and the temperature on an ivy-covered wall can be up to 36 percent lower than on a bare wall.

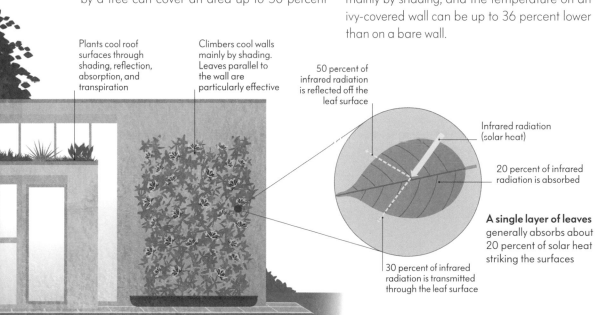

Plants cool roof surfaces through shading, reflection, absorption, and transpiration

Climbers cool walls mainly by shading. Leaves parallel to the wall are particularly effective

50 percent of infrared radiation is reflected off the leaf surface

Infrared radiation (solar heat)

20 percent of infrared radiation is absorbed

A single layer of leaves generally absorbs about 20 percent of solar heat striking the surfaces

30 percent of infrared radiation is transmitted through the leaf surface

KEEP YOUR HOME NATURALLY COOL

If you do have space for a tree, choose one that has a broad crown or arching form, such as oak or silver birch. The denser the canopy, the deeper the shade the tree will cast and the cooler the ground beneath it. These natural pergolas will provide shade for sitting under while still allowing views into the garden. A clearance of at least 8ft (2.4m) from the ground to the lowest branches will allow plenty of room for people to move beneath.

Shady types

Make sure you provide good growing conditions, as many trees need to be actively transpiring to be effective at cooling—transpiration consumes solar energy. If the roots are growing in compacted or badly aerated soil, transpiration can be reduced by a factor of five.

If you're growing a tree for shading your house wall, a tree with plenty of leaf cover, such as Midland hawthorn or Japanese dogwood, will be effective. Consider whether you want a deciduous tree that will allow winter sun through and so help to keep surfaces warmer in the colder months (see pp.168–171).

Plant at a safe distance

Most trees planted close to buildings cause no damage. However, in drought conditions, trees growing in shrinkable clay soils can dry out the soil below foundations, causing the soil to shrink. This can result in subsidence of the foundations and structural cracking. If drains are not watertight, tree roots can grow into them, causing blockages. To avoid such problems, opt for trees with the lowest water demands, such as catalpa, magnolia, sweet gum, and hazel.

Green up your roof

Rooftops can often be the hottest surfaces, particularly in cities. Covering them with plants not only helps to cool individual buildings, it can also help to reduce the air temperature of the city itself. Green roofs differ from ornamental roof gardens, which are planted much like ground-level gardens in planters and flower beds. Plants on green roofs grow in a lightweight substrate, or growing medium, laid over the roof membrane. The first green roofs, known as extensive roofs, were planted with low-maintenance plants such as stonecrops and

You don't need lots of space to enjoy the shade from trees (left). Small trees and tall shrubs can provide cooling shade in a sunny courtyard garden.

Green roofs (right) can be low maintenance and usually don't need to be irrigated, except when they're first established.

grasses, but now there are also semiextensive systems that have deeper layers of substrate, allowing a wider range of plants to grow.

Recent studies show that, as well as insulating buildings, green roofs reduce water run-off, trap air pollutants, absorb noise, and provide extra habitats for wildlife. If you want to focus on biodiversity, you would need a rubble-based substrate and various natural features such as mounds of sand, stones, and logs for creatures to live in. Always consider the weight and structural load of green roofs.

Scientists are experimenting to find out which plants can cope best with the windy, exposed conditions and also provide the best cooling. Green-roof specialists can advise which kind of roof is best for your needs.

SHADY TYPES

These trees are good choices for shading your garden or house wall.

EVERGREEN

- **Evergreen magnolia** (*Magnolia grandiflora*)
- **Portugal laurel** (*Prunus lusitanica*)

DECIDUOUS

- **Midland hawthorn** (*Crataegus laevigata*)
- **Japanese dogwood** (*Cornus kousa*)
- **Hupeh crab** (*Malus hupehensis*)

Save energy with plants

Insulate your walls and roof outside as well as inside to beat winter cold.

In temperate climates, heating is the main consumer of energy. You can reduce energy costs not only by insulating the inside of your building but also the outside. Shelter belts of trees will cut down windchill and so reduce the heat transfer from building façades into the colder atmosphere. Climbers, living walls, and green roofs can also provide protective layers in winter.

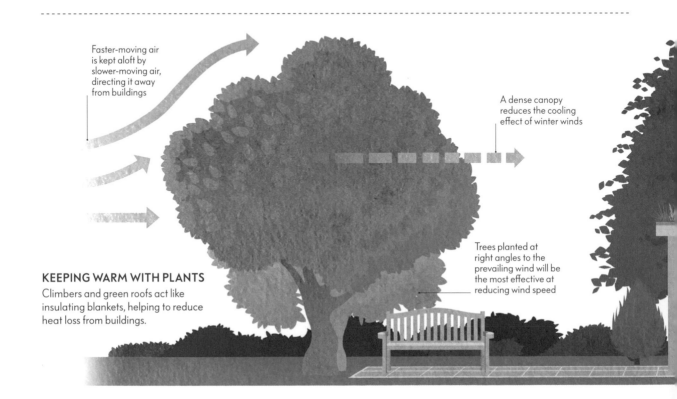

Faster-moving air is kept aloft by slower-moving air, directing it away from buildings

A dense canopy reduces the cooling effect of winter winds

Trees planted at right angles to the prevailing wind will be the most effective at reducing wind speed

KEEPING WARM WITH PLANTS
Climbers and green roofs act like insulating blankets, helping to reduce heat loss from buildings.

GREEN BARRIERS AGAINST THE COLD

Block the cold with insulating layers, such as a climber grown directly against a wall or on a frame, a living wall, or a green roof. Alternatively, if you have space, use a line of trees to cut the wind speed. Even a single tree can help to reduce the chilling effects of wind on a building

Trees to cut the chill

Windchill is a key factor in heat loss in buildings. A simulation study of an office building in Scotland suggested that planting a shelter belt of trees to block the prevailing wind close to buildings could result in energy savings of 18 percent. Trees not only reduce the wind speed, but also act as a barrier to minimize heat loss from buildings at night. The deciduous trees in the Scottish study allowed the brick wall surface to absorb solar radiation on sunny days, raising the temperature of the wall. Even trees without leaves can still help to slow down the wind.

Cozy up to green

Climbers, living walls, and green roofs create a barrier against cold air and wind that would otherwise enter the building through cracks and holes. They also trap a layer of warmer air behind their leaves, which slows down the rate of heat transfer from the inside to the outside.

A study of green ivy façades in the UK showed that, in winter, the surface of a building under an 8in- (20cm-) thick layer of ivy can be on average 7°F (3.8°C) warmer than a bare wall.

A green roof provides a layer of insulation, reducing the heat escaping from the building

Climbers create an insulating barrier against wind and cold air

A 2017 Canadian study found that **removing the trees from around buildings** would **increase** the building's **energy consumption** in **winter** by **10 percent**

GREEN WALL INSULATION

There are a number of different types of green walls. A self-attaching climber planted in the ground or in a planter is known as direct greening. A climber trained on a trellis or wire is known as indirect greening. A living wall system has pockets or planter boxes installed on the wall to support a selection of plants that are not necessarily climbers.

Greening up the walls

The easiest and cheapest way to make a green wall is simply to plant a climber or wall shrub next to a wall. You could also consider training a fruit tree as an espalier or fan against a wall (see pp.156–157). Attaching wires or trellis to the wall for climbers to use creates a gap of insulating air between the plants and the building. If you want to cover an entire exterior wall, you may need professional help with the installation of supports.

Living wall art

Living wall systems are an exciting way to green up buildings. They range from simple fabric planters that you can attach to a frame or directly to a wall and fill with plants, to large modular systems connected to a drip-irrigation system that usually have to be installed by a professional.

Living wall systems can support a selection of different plants, such as ferns, grasses, herbs, annuals, perennials, fruit, and vegetables. You can use your creativity to arrange them in eye-catching displays of living art.

For balconies and smaller areas, rows of pockets or modules that can be attached to the wall are ideal. Fill these with potting soil for an inexpensive and space-saving way of growing ornamentals and edible plants. Unless you have space to install a drip-irrigation system, you will need to water by hand, so choose plants that have similar requirements to make watering simpler.

Professional installers construct engineered systems in layers. They attach irrigated planting modules to a frame that is separated from the building with an air gap and geotextile membrane, trapping pockets of warmer air in winter. Some suppliers now offer modules planted specifically to attract pollinating insects.

Interior green walls are also a good option. Modular walls fitted with water reservoirs to reduce their maintenance requirements are becoming more widely available. Your choice of plants will depend on the amount of light and heat exposure they will experience.

> In winter, **a living wall** can **reduce** a building's **heating** demands **by 4 percent**

Plant sun-loving species near the top of your wall, with shade-tolerant ones at the base. If your wall gets sun for less than half the day, choose plants for shade.

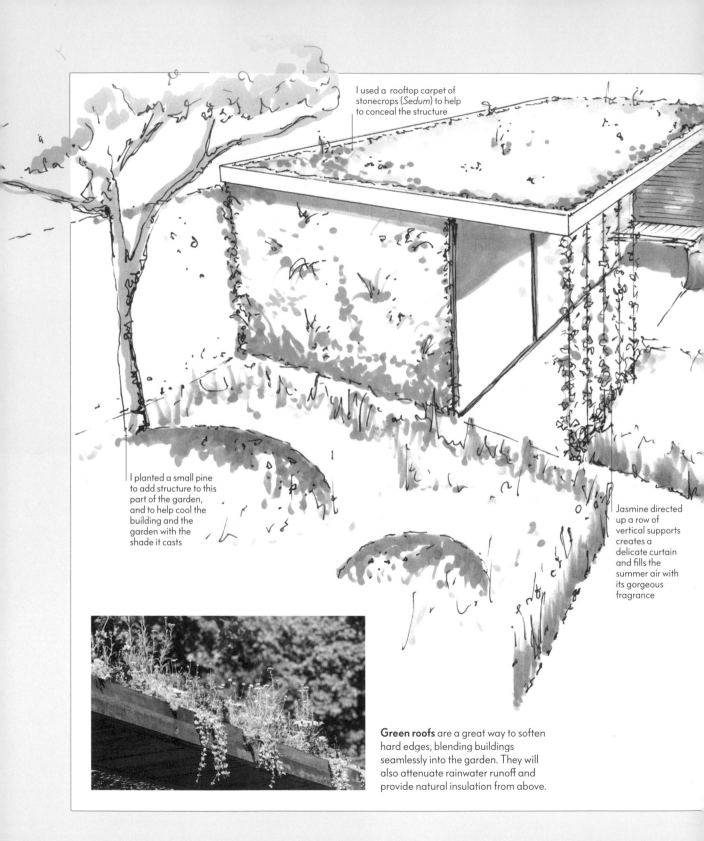

I used a rooftop carpet of stonecrops (*Sedum*) to help to conceal the structure

I planted a small pine to add structure to this part of the garden, and to help cool the building and the garden with the shade it casts

Jasmine directed up a row of vertical supports creates a delicate curtain and fills the summer air with its gorgeous fragrance

Green roofs are a great way to soften hard edges, blending buildings seamlessly into the garden. They will also attenuate rainwater runoff and provide natural insulation from above.

Greening a garden room

Vertical planting and green roofs are a great way to add interest to buildings and to insulate and shade them, and are also a clever way to introduce more plants into the garden. Aside from being practical, greenery on buildings can soften hard architectural edges and highlight textures. Old buildings in particular can look rather brutal, but they can be softened or even masked by introducing some texture through planting.

Garden buildings can be purely functional storage areas or lovely places to retreat to for contemplation, to recharge, or just to immerse yourself in nature. When introducing textures, contrasting elements can be extremely effective, such as the smooth, architectural lines of walls and corners clothed in undulating climbers, or the angular geometry of a roof offset by a soft green and gray carpet of stonecrops.

Climbers, such as jasmine, can be used to veil an unsightly building if they are trained up vertical wires or a trellis attached to the walls. Ivy, wisteria, or honeysuckle are other good choices.

Living walls are an attractive and clever way to introduce greenery to vertical spaces.

Future-proofing for drought

More frequent dry spells are putting stress on our water supplies, but a little planning will keep your garden healthy.

Creating a drought-tolerant garden doesn't mean that you have to dig up your existing garden and start again—a few tweaks and changes can keep it looking beautiful without constant watering. Cultivating your soil to maximize its water retention, choosing plants carefully for your soil and site, thinking about alternative methods of maintaining a lawn, and investigating sustainable ways to use water supplies can all help to keep your garden healthy when temperatures peak and water is scarce.

HOW CAN PLANTS BE WATER EFFICIENT?

With global warming predicted to increase by 0.36°F (0.2°C) every decade, many gardeners will feel the impact of climate change as water shortages and hosepipe bans become more common. Agriculture, industry, and homes are using more water, placing a strain on the environment and water supplies. In some countries, gardens use more than 50 percent of household water in summer.

So why is drought a such a problem? During really dry spells, some plants lose water through their leaves faster than they can absorb it through their roots. Over an extended period, this disrupts the plant's ability to carry out vital processes, such as photosynthesis (converting sunlight into chemical energy for plant growth) and transpiration (transporting water from roots to leaves to be released as water vapor). Plants suffering from drought-stress become weaker, don't grow well, and may become susceptible to disease or not recover. Reducing your water usage, collecting rainwater, choosing drought-tolerant and water-efficient plants, and using new technologies can all help your garden cope with dry spells.

BLUEPRINT FOR WATER EFFICIENCY

Current knowledge suggests that for a fruit tree to be highly water-efficient, it needs to be small with relatively few leaves, have been grafted onto a dwarf rootstock to limit the size of its canopy, and need less water compared with larger trees that have more extensive root systems.

Choose a tree with a low leaf-area index (see p.22). A tree with fewer leaves may lose less water than a tree with a high leaf-area index

Add a mulch layer to lock moisture in the soil, preventing water loss from surface evaporation and helping to keep soil cooler (see p.181)

Choose trees with an open canopy. A lighter, airier covering of leaves will allow sunlight to penetrate, encouraging photosynthesis, and boost growth and fruit production

Select a water-efficient plant that shows fewer signs of stress during times of drought—water-efficient fruit trees can continue to produce fruit, for instance

Grow on a dwarf rootstock. Plants can be grafted onto the root of a smaller variety to limit canopy size and reduce water requirements

Use a drip-irrigation system to reduce ground evaporation, encourage deeper rooting, and improve drought resilience (see p.181).

Right plant, right place

Even closely related plants can cope differently with dry spells. For example, research in South African orchards compared the water efficiency of two types of apple trees ('Cripps Pink' and 'Golden Delicious'). The water efficiency of a fruit tree can be measured by how much fruit it produces (in lbs) per 264 gallons (1,000 litres) of water used. 'Cripps Pink' trees, with more open canopies and fewer leaves, used less water and had higher yields of fruit than 'Golden Delicious'.

European countries use an average of **38 gallons (144 litres)** of water **per person** per day

PLANTING FOR DROUGHT RESISTANCE

Plants have different strategies for dealing with extreme heat (see opposite), and it is plants with these characteristics that you want to include in your garden. By choosing drought-tolerant plants for the driest areas in your plot, you can have a beautiful garden and be water-wise.

This doesn't mean switching only to plants found in the desert: there are many species,

Many plants thrive in arid environments, relishing free-draining soils on slopes that would be otherwise difficult to plant.

DROUGHT-TOLERANT CHARACTERISTICS

Identifying drought-tolerant plants is easy when you know what to look for. This list will help you spot those most likely to survive dry conditions:

1 Gray-green or silver leaves Pale foliage helps reflect hot solar rays, as in species such as common wormwood (*Artemisia absinthium*).

2 Aromatic leaves These contain volatile oils thought to cool foliage as they evaporate, reducing water loss; try species such as rue (*Ruta graveolens*).

3 Fleshy leaves or stems These allow water to be stored inside; houseleeks (*Sempervivum*) have dramatic forms.

4 Hairy leaves Fine hairs help trap moisture and reduce the drying effect of wind, in plants such as common sage (*Salvia officinalis*).

including trees, flowering perennials, shrubs, climbers, grasses, and bulbs, that cope well with drought and need little or no water.

Some like it hot

Certain plants are specifically adapted to dry conditions: some have deep taproots (the main part of the plant's root system) or widely spreading roots; others fold or shed their leaves, or shut down the stomata (leaf pores) in order to conserve water. Mediterranean plants are ideal (but need good drainage), and those with gray-green or silver leaves are good choices, as they reflect the sun's hot rays, conserving moisture.

Succulents store water inside their leaves or stems and are good low-water plants for containers of all sizes. Their architectural forms and subtle foliage colors mean they provide all-year interest, and the hardiest types, such as stonecrops and houseleeks, can survive outdoors in winter even in temperate climates. More tender succulents, such as echeveria and aloes, are better suited to urban and coastal gardens, and should be brought indoors over winter in colder areas.

Give plants the best start

The plants you choose should be appropriate for your soil and aspect. Before you plant, cultivate your soil (see p.136) to improve its water retention, and ensure it is free-draining—dig grit into heavy soils to prevent roots getting waterlogged in winter. Once planted, apply a mulch and top with a layer of grit or stone chippings to prevent moisture loss. If your garden is on a slope, position plants in the highest, sunniest spots, or create a raised site on free-draining soil.

A LAWN TO BEAT THE HEAT

For many people, lawns are a quintessential element in a garden. Lawns can also have environmental benefits by absorbing noise and air pollutants, and offering a mini habitat to insects and birds probing for food. The old advice for keeping lawns green was to water them liberally in the summer, and add regular doses of synthetic fertilizer and weedkiller, but research shows overwatering can make grass less drought-tolerant, and with drier summers and water shortages forecast for the future, it's time for a better, more sustainable approach.

Resilient grass

By making simple changes you can still have lush, green lawns and be water-efficient. In temperate regions, grass can turn brown and stop growing during hot spells. However, a lawn that contains drought-tolerant, native grass species such as fescues should green up again after a dry spell—the roots of tall fescue can extend up to 3ft (1m) deep to access moisture. Look for turf or seed that has these grass mixes. In the arid regions of North America, native grasses such as buffalo grass (*Bouteloua dactyloides*) and blue grama (*Bouteloua gracilis*) need little or no water. In dry regions of southern France, dense *Zoysia* grass survives with no summer watering and turns brown in winter.

Letting your grass grow longer during hot weather encourages it to have deeper, denser roots, enabling it to survive longer without rain, so raise the cutting height on your mower if you can. Don't bother to rake up clippings in hot condtions: leaving a thin layer of cuttings on the lawn will slow water evaporation and add nutrients. Mulching mowers are specifically designed for this. Aerate your lawn by making holes at regular intervals using a garden fork to allow water, air, and nutrients to get to the roots more easily.

Barely there lawns

Try switching to a low-maintenance lawn that requires no mowing and little watering—or sow wildflowers and let your grass grow long like a meadow, or plant seasonal bulbs for spikes of color. You could also mow only where you most use your lawn and let it grow longer elsewhere.

If you intend to water your lawn, consider reducing the lawn area to cut down on water use. Replace grass with thyme to reduce the amount of watering needed or reshape the lawn to allow space for a gravel garden, a drought-tolerant border, or areas of decking.

Sprinklers can use up to **238 gallons (900 liters)** of water **per hour**

To reduce water demands, consider replacing all or part of your lawn with groundcover that can tolerate light pedestrian traffic, such as this thyme.

Save water by letting part of your lawn grow long and plant bulbs for splashes of color throughout the seasons.

Long grass planted with wildflowers will not need a lot of watering. You can mow a strip through your wildflower meadow for access.

BE WATER-WISE IN THE GARDEN

Water demand is expected to outstrip supply over the next 50 years, but there are many ways you can reduce pressure on water supplies and help to prevent this scenario. Store rainwater, use it wisely, and help plants maximize water uptake in dry periods.

Capture nature's resources

By collecting rainwater, you can have thriving plants even in times of drought and during watering bans, reduce the demand on water supplies, and save money on water bills. You can also use your rainwater to top up your pond, if you have one. Wildlife ponds, in particular, should be filled with rainwater (see p.56).

The easiest way to capture rainwater is by attaching a rain barrel to the downpipe of your house. Studies show that even in dry areas, 6,340 gallons (24,000 litres) can be collected from the roof of an average house in one year. There are also wall-mounted rain catchers that can work well in small spaces and on balconies. You can also capture water from sheds and other outbuildings by installing gutters and downpipes that flow into rain catchers.

Rain barrels can range from rustic wood to sleek metal. You can upcycle any watertight vessel to collect water, and custom rain catchers have airtight lids (which prevent insects from breeding in the water) and taps near the base.

Don't forget to use your gray water, too. This is water that has already been used, such as that from baths, showers, washing machine rinse cycles, and sinks. You can siphon it off using a hose, or scoop it up in buckets and pour it on ornamental plants (but not edibles). Always use gray water immediately to minimize the growth of bacteria.

Make every drop count

When water is scarce, you want it to reach plants directly, losing as little as possible to evaporation. Do this by planting in soil with plenty of organic matter to retain moisture and by mulching (see p.136). If you are growing in containers, select potting compost to suit the type of plant: for short-lived varieties, use multipurpose, peat-free potting compost; for permanent and established plants, use soil-based compost with nutrients. You can add

grit into the mix for species that prefer free-draining conditions.

If you are planting in the ground, you may need to improve the soil first by mixing in generous quantities of organic matter, such as garden compost, well-rotted manure, or mushroom compost (see p.136), to help the soil retain moisture without becoming waterlogged. Research has found that spreading a layer of organic matter onto damp soil reduces evaporation from the soil surface by up to 75 percent. It also helps the soil beneath stay cooler—by up to 10°C (18°F) on hot days—so the plants are less likely to need additional water. Mulches suppress weeds, reducing the competition for moisture, and add nutrients to the soil as they decompose.

Water well, but not too often

During hot, dry weather, provide enough water to keep plants alive but not so much that you encourage them to produce new growth, which has high water needs. Frequent watering causes plants to keep their roots close to the surface, where they are likely to dry out, instead of delving deeper into the soil for moisture.

Seep hoses dug into the soil direct water straight to roots and mean no loss of water through evaporation, as does a drip-irrigation system (see box). Both systems can be attached to rain barrels—automatic systems should link to soil moisture sensors. Alternatively, you could put plants in planters attached to a surface to make a living wall that is relatively easy to water.

Living walls make an attractive feature, and you can irrigate them with built-in water reservoirs, by using a drip-irrigation system, or with a seep hose.

Water-wise techniques

- Water generously and then let the soil dry out before watering again.
- Direct water to the roots, rather than sprinkling it on the leaves and around the plant.
- Water in the early morning or toward the end of the day, or even at night on a timer linked to a water probe, to reduce water loss by evaporation.
- Only water established turf when the soil is dry— once every seven to 10 days is plenty.
- Plants in pots and hanging baskets need more frequent watering than those growing in the ground, as their roots cannot spread as far to access water and nutrients. Containers with built-in reservoirs use water efficiently, allowing it to be drawn up according to the plant's needs.
- Use a drip-irrigation system. Slow, deep delivery of water to the root zone reduces ground evaporation, encourages deeper rooting, and improves drought resilience. Drip-irrigation systems linked to moisture sensors in the soil only deliver water if the plants need it.
- In extreme heat, shade nets reduce evaporation and transpiration from leaves.

BETH CHATTO'S GRAVEL GARDEN
Take inspiration from Beth Chatto's renowned gravel garden, where the drought-loving purple-pink vervain and allium flowers and their striking seedheads add color to swaths of *Stipa* grasses in the middle distance.

Make your garden a no-flood zone

Protect your home and the environment from water damage and pollution with some simple preventative strategies.

Many experts believe that the changing climate is causing more frequent and more intense heavy rainfall events, which cause flooding. Paved drives, patios, and other surfaces prevent natural drainage, forcing surface water to run off and cause flash flooding. In some areas, sewage also enters rivers and oceans after a storm, as drains spill their contents into waterways. You can help to counter these effects in your garden by installing permeable surfaces, collecting rain, and selecting plants that soak up and filter storm water.

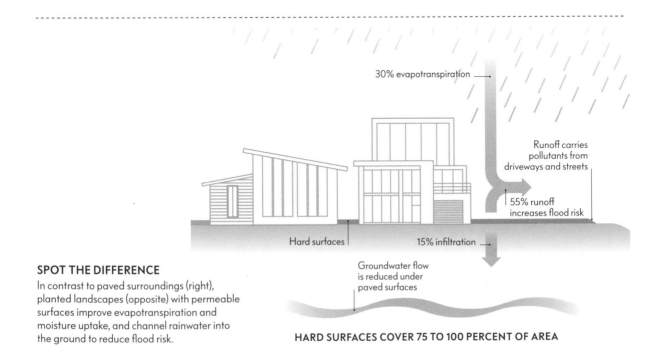

30% evapotranspiration

Runoff carries pollutants from driveways and streets

55% runoff increases flood risk

Hard surfaces

15% infiltration

Groundwater flow is reduced under paved surfaces

SPOT THE DIFFERENCE
In contrast to paved surroundings (right), planted landscapes (opposite) with permeable surfaces improve evapotranspiration and moisture uptake, and channel rainwater into the ground to reduce flood risk.

HARD SURFACES COVER 75 TO 100 PERCENT OF AREA

HOW PLANTS PREVENT FLOODING

Paving, tarmac, concrete, and other hard, non-permeable landscaping materials increase the volume of rainwater that runs off gardens by up to 50 percent, making the risk of flooding more common. The impact, both to the environment and our homes and businesses, is high; in the UK alone, the cost of flood damage and coastal erosion is an estimated $1.3 billion a year.

So what actually happens to the water that flows from our properties during a storm? Rainwater on roofs collects into gutters and downspouts, and from there runs into sinks—rubble-filled holes underground that allow water to filter through the earth—or into stormwater sewers in the street. The sewers then channel this untreated rainwater, together with any runoff from gardens and streets, directly into waterways, such as rivers and seas. Rainwater picks up pollutants as it flows along the ground, including animal waste, engine oil, and detergents, which also wash into sewer systems and waterways. During a downpour, the volume of rainwater can overwhelm drainage systems, causing localized floods, and in areas where wastewater from toilets and sinks mixes with rainwater, untreated sewage may flood into gardens, homes, rivers, and seas.

To prevent too much water entering overstretched sewers in the first place, the solution is simple: pull up the paving and start planting instead.

The botanical flood barrier

All plants soak up water through their roots, but some plants are much more efficient at it than others. Trees, especially those with large, leafy canopies and extensive root systems, not only draw in and store vast amounts of water, but their roots also provide natural gaps and channels deep in the earth, allowing rainfall to move and filter through the ground, instead of running off the surface and causing floods.

The difference plants make is quite astonishing. In a garden consisting of 80–90 percent plant cover, the soil absorbs about 42 percent of total rainfall. A further 38–40 percent is transferred from the land to the atmosphere by evaporation from the soil and other surfaces and by transpiration from plants, a process known as evapotranspiration. Some plants (see p.139) and soil types also filter pollutants, ensuring that fewer toxins wash into the environment.

In contrast, where hard surfaces account for 75–100 percent of a garden, only 15 percent of the rainwater is absorbed into the ground, while 55 percent runs off into street drainage systems or stays on the surface, greatly increasing flood risk.

38% evapotranspiration

Runoff is held and filtered by soil and plants before entering waterways

20% runoff

42% infiltration

Groundwater flow is increased under planted landscapes

PLANTS COVER 80 TO 90 PERCENT OF AREA

HOW PLANTS CAPTURE WATER

More than half of the human body consists of water, but this pales in comparison to plants, whose water content can be above 90 percent. It's no wonder plants need huge volumes of water to stay alive. Once their roots absorb water, it is then drawn up through veinlike vessels in their stems into leaves, flowers, seeds, and fruits.

Plants retain only a fraction of the water they absorb for growth and development. Any excess is released as water vapor through tiny pores called stomata located in leaves, needles, and stems. Known as transpiration, this process is the plant's method of responding to its environment, the weather, and soil conditions, regulating the amount of water it releases or retains to grow and survive.

Slowing and trapping rainfall

Plants also physically trap rainwater on their stems and leaves, and some of this moisture then evaporates back into the atmosphere without ever hitting the ground. In addition, foliage and branches slow down the rate at which rain falls, allowing the soil more time to absorb it and reducing the runoff that causes flooding. The rough or hairy leaves of species such as lungwort, hydrangea, and hawthorn are highly effective at trapping water droplets, forming yet another barrier and reducing the volume of water that actually hits the ground.

Some trees can take up **200 gallons (900 liters) of water** a day; **98 percent** of it **transpires** into the **atmosphere**

Rapid responders

Plants with highly responsive stomata adapt quickly to changing conditions—for example, during storms—making them ideal for flood-prone gardens. Stomata open not only to allow water vapor to escape, but also to let in carbon dioxide, which is essential for photosynthesis—the process by which plants make food. While all plants' stomata open and close in response to temperature, water levels, and light, some react more quickly than others. Rapid responders include trees such as ginkgo, hornbeam, and hawthorn, whose stomata open wide during warm periods after rainfall, but close again quickly when drier conditions return in order to reduce water loss and prevent wilting.

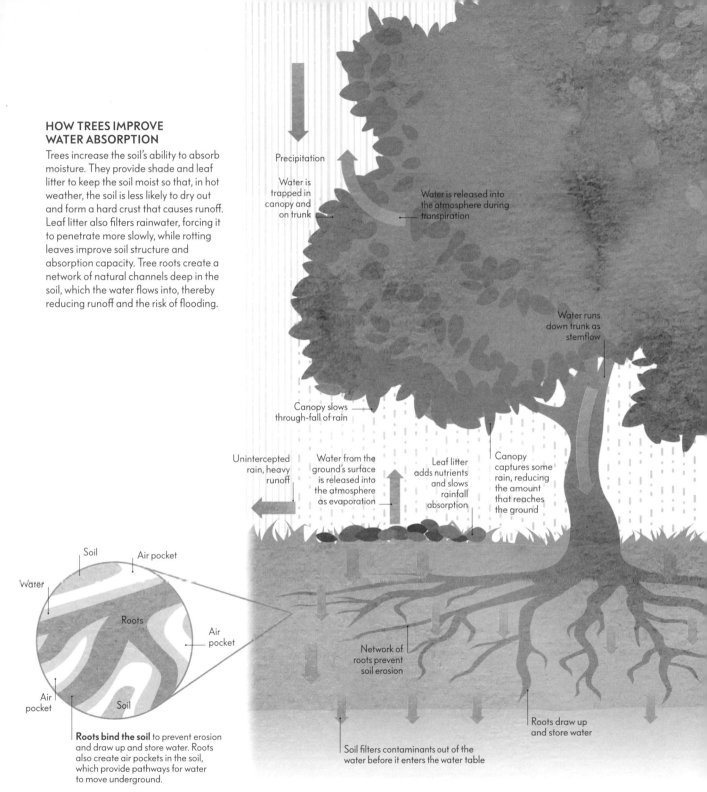

HOW TREES IMPROVE WATER ABSORPTION

Trees increase the soil's ability to absorb moisture. They provide shade and leaf litter to keep the soil moist so that, in hot weather, the soil is less likely to dry out and form a hard crust that causes runoff. Leaf litter also filters rainwater, forcing it to penetrate more slowly, while rotting leaves improve soil structure and absorption capacity. Tree roots create a network of natural channels deep in the soil, which the water flows into, thereby reducing runoff and the risk of flooding.

Precipitation

Water is trapped in canopy and on trunk

Water is released into the atmosphere during transpiration

Water runs down trunk as stemflow

Canopy slows through-fall of rain

Unintercepted rain, heavy runoff

Water from the ground's surface is released into the atmosphere as evaporation

Leaf litter adds nutrients and slows rainfall absorption

Canopy captures some rain, reducing the amount that reaches the ground

Soil

Air pocket

Water

Roots

Air pocket

Air pocket

Soil

Network of roots prevent soil erosion

Roots draw up and store water

Soil filters contaminants out of the water before it enters the water table

Roots bind the soil to prevent erosion and draw up and store water. Roots also create air pockets in the soil, which provide pathways for water to move underground.

MAKE A FLOOD-PROOF GARDEN

No matter how large or small it may be, a flood-resistant garden should include as many plants as possible. If you have room, plant a small tree or two, but if space is tight, shrubs, perennials, and a layer of groundcover plants will all absorb rainwater, drastically reducing the amount of runoff into drains in the street. A hedge between your garden and a road will take up water, while also filtering out dust and pollutants (see pp.20–29), thereby decreasing the volume of runoff. All these measures will contribute to sustainable urban drainage.

You can also attach a trellis or wires to fences and walls to provide support for leafy climbers, and even a few planted pots around the door or on a patio will absorb some rainfall. Also consider installing a green roof of easy-care succulents on a garage or outbuilding—seek professional advice first to check that your roof is suitable and that plants will thrive.

Replace hard surfaces

Swap paving slabs and concrete for permeable landscaping, such as gravel, grasscrete (a semi-permeable material that grass can grow through), or bricks bedded into sand, for paths and drives. Keep parking areas to a minimum by calculating how much you really need, then include hard landscaping only where the vehicles will drive in and park. For example, you could use just two strips of permeable paving for the car wheels to run along, and plant the space in between. Species such as moneywort or creeping thyme are ideal, as they can cope with occasional bruising and shade.

Capture water to reduce runoff

Rain barrels are an excellent way to capture and store excess water from roofs (see p.180). They reduce the volume of runoff in the garden, as well as providing free water to irrigate your plants during dry spells.

Even the tiniest garden can act as an effective natural flood barrier. Interplant paving with a groundcover such as thyme to soak up rainfall.

Decorate decks by installing planters that not only soften the feel and look of the space, but provide several botanical "sponges" to absorb rainwater.

Install a green roof on garden structures, such as bike or bin storage, to help absorb rainfall. Stonecrops are a good choice, as they are hardy and require little maintenance.

Let the ground breathe with permeable landscaping, such as gravel, slate chips, and bark, which allow water to drain into, not run off, the ground.

CREATE A SIMPLE RAIN GARDEN

Rain gardens offer a natural solution for managing water runoff in areas prone to surface flooding because they capture, store, and filter rainwater. These low-maintenance gardens absorb 30 percent more rainfall than a lawn and usually require no watering once the plants are established. By selecting a wide range of plants, you can also increase the number of insects, birds, and other wildlife visiting your garden, bringing benefits all around.

Slow drainage to reduce runoff

To make a rain garden, you first need to create one or two wide depressions, similar to shallow ponds, and fill them with plants (see opposite). During a shower or storm, rain flows into these depressions from surfaces such as patios, paths, and driveways. The rain garden holds the water before it slowly drains into the soil or is taken up by the plants, with little or no runoff into drains.

If you have space, you can make things even more efficient by installing a shallow trench or channel to link your roof's downpipe to the rain garden. You will need to seek professional advice for this, and the depression must have a diameter equal to at least 20 percent of the total roof area in order to accommodate all the runoff. Also get advice if you have a high water table, a steeply sloping plot, or a septic system.

Site your rain garden at least 10ft (3m) away from your home to avoid damaging its foundations. It should be at the bottom of a gentle incline, where water naturally pools when it rains. Locate any underground pipes and cables, such as those for gas and electricity, before digging. Mark out your rain garden and remove any vegetation, such as turf.

Preparing the site

Dig a saucer-shaped hole up to 18in (45cm) deep with sloping sides and a flat base. You'll need a deeper hole— 24in (60cm)—in clay soil, as the depression will retain water for longer. Use some of the excavated soil to make a berm—a ridge along the sides and lower edge of the hole to help contain the water. The berm must be about 1ft (30cm) wide and at least 4in (10cm) higher than ground level. Make a channel to carry the water to the rain garden. Create a gravel-filled channel or use a pipe to direct any overspill into a conventional drainage system, such as a soakaway, drain, or pond.

Next, stock the garden with plants suitable for your site and climate, and choose those that are capable of withstanding both waterlogged conditions as well as dry spells.

You may also want to consider adding other water-capturing features to your garden, such as a rain barrel or a wildlife pond (see pp.56–57).

A **rain garden** measuring **a fifth** of the **roof area** it serves can usually **manage** all the **runoff** from a typical **storm**

RAIN-GARDEN PLANTS

Choose plants that are suited to the conditions in your garden, such as the amount of sun or shade it receives.

PLANTS FOR WATER TOLERANCE

Put plants that can cope with occasional waterlogging near the inlet channel and in the base.

- **Black-eyed Susans** (*Rudbeckia hirta*)
- **Bugleweed** (*Ajuga reptans*)
- **Clustered bellflower** (*Campanula glomerata*)
- **Maiden grass** (*Miscanthus sinensis*)
- **False spirea** (*Astilbe* species)
- **Hostas**
- **Irises** (*Iris ensata, I. sibirica*)
- **Geranium 'ROZANNE'** ('Germat')
- **Sneezeweed** (*Helenium* species)
- **Valentine flower** (*Crocosmia* 'Lucifer')

LARGER PLANTS FOR DRIER AREAS

- **Barberry** (*Berberis*)
- **Butterfly bush** (*Buddleja*)
- **Common dogwood** (*Cornus sanguinea*)
- **Elder** (*Sambucus*)
- **Flowering currant** (*Ribes*)
- **Forsythia**
- **Guelder rose** (*Viburnum opulus*)
- **Hemp agrimony** (*Eupatorium cannabinum*)
- **Mallow** (*Lavatera*)
- **Mock-orange** (*Philadelphus*)
- **Serviceberry** (*Amelanchier*)
- **St. John's wort** (*Hypericum*)
- **Smoke bush** (*Cotinus*)

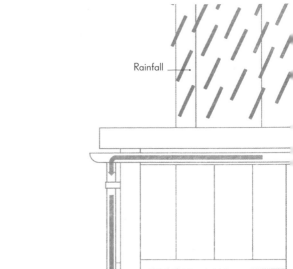

Rainfall

Rainwater runoff

Connecting channel for downspout

Plants that can cope with wet and dry conditions will need very little maintenance after they are established

Berm to help to contain water

Loose soil absorbs and filters the runoff, removing pollutants

A SIMPLE RAIN GARDEN

Choose a site for your rain garden in full sun or partial shade and at the base of a gentle incline—10 percent or less—where it will collect rainwater from hard surfaces or from a downpipe.

Outlet pipe to sink, drain, or pond

Water percolates slowly through soil around plant roots

Designing a rain garden

As a changing climate threatens our planet, our individual contributions to protect the environment are important. Something as simple as creating a rain garden or a permeable driveway can have a significant impact. As well as being sustainable and beneficial for the environment, rain gardens make functional spaces attractive and can be fun to plan.

Create an area that directs rainwater through the soil and back into the water table. Include beds of moisture-loving perennials around paved surfaces and plant groundcovers and creeping perennials between paving stones to allow rainwater to drain away through the soil. This prevents runoff from hard surfaces going directly into the drainage system after downpours, which contributes to flooding. A rain chain is an efficient way to direct water into a rain barrel, and you can use the captured rainwater to water plants.

Don't waste valuable roof water. Often ornamental in appearance, rain chains are a great way to direct water from the roof into a planted bed or a rain barrel for collection.

Permeable driveways (left) are an attractive, sustainable option compared to their concrete or paved counterparts.

Spreading perennials such as bugleweed (right) and golden creeping Jenny (far right) are good choices for planting on a driveway.

I planted moisture-loving perennials, such as Siberian iris and purple loosestrife, to provide a colorful border next to the paved area

Plant groundcovers, such as thyme, between paving stones or use a permeable material such as gravel

Some mat-forming and compact spreading perennials, such as storksbill (*Erodium* x *variabile* 'Roseum') and golden creeping Jenny, will tolerate moderate foot traffic

Plant a haven for pollinators

Insect pollinators, including bees and moths, are in decline, but you can help by creating an attractive habitat for them.

We rely on pollinators for the majority of our food crops, yet pollinating insect populations are in trouble. You can help boost their falling numbers by making your garden a little patch of pollinator paradise that meets their needs. Attract pollinators with pollen-bearing, nectar-rich flowers that bloom at different times of year, and with night-scented plants and larval food plants for butterfly and moth caterpillars, and provide plenty of places for pollinators to shelter.

POLLINATORS IN PERIL

Studies show that pollinators are disappearing fast, with up to 50 percent of all bee species threatened in some European countries. Loss of habitat, a changing climate, pesticides, and the spread of pests and diseases are all thought to be contributing factors. The *Varroa* mite can weaken honeybee colonies, and many wild pollinators, such as bumblebees and solitary bees, are also in decline—three species of bumblebee have become extinct in the UK in recent decades. And it's not just bees that are disappearing—in the UK alone, more than half the butterfly and moth species have declined over the past 50 years.

Recent research shows that moths—such as this elephant hawkmoth feeding on a red campion growing in a wildflower meadow—are important pollinators.

Most apple trees need insects for pollination.

INSECT-POLLINATED PLANTS

Many fruits and vegetables need to be pollinated by insects.

FRUITS

- **Strawberry** (*Fragaria × ananassa*)
- **Apple** (*Malus domestica*)
- **Blueberry** (*Vaccinium corymbosum*)
- **Raspberry** (*Rubus idaeus*)
- **Cranberry** (*Vaccinium oxycoccos*)

VEGETABLES

- **Fava beans** (*Vicia faba*)
- **Peas** (*Pisum sativum*)
- **Zucchini** (*Cucurbita pepo*)
- **Broccoli** (*Brassica oleracea* var. *italica*)
- **Onion** (*Allium cepa*)
- **Asparagus** (*Asparagus officinalis*)

The crucial role of pollinators

Globally, bees are critical pollinators of food crops, with the honeybee pollinating 70 of about 100 crop species that feed 90 percent of the world. Pollination is also essential for crops, such as field beans and clover, to feed the livestock we farm for meat and milk. The products of pollination (seeds, berries, and fruit) help to feed many other animals in the food chain and maintain the genetic diversity of flowering plants. If pollinators disappeared, so would many of the plants that rely exclusively on them for pollination.

Close to home

However, it's not all bad news. Urban gardens in North America and Europe can support higher densities of bumblebees and solitary bees than farmed land does, and bee species that feed on a wide range of plants are thriving. You can help pollinators by using plants to attract these important insects to your garden.

Some plants are pollinated by wind or water, but many rely on animals to transfer pollen from the male to the female parts of flowers, enabling plants to set seeds and fruit. Some of these pollinators are large creatures, such as bats or birds, but most are insects, such as bees, flies, wasps, beetles, butterflies, and moths. It's this army of insects that pollinate many of the edibles in our gardens and community spaces.

Most pollinating insects, such as bees, visit flowers for a nutritional reward of nectar (a sugar-rich liquid), pollen (a source of protein), or both. Adult butterflies and moths take only nectar, sucking it up through their proboscis.

A number of vegetable plants rely on insect pollination, too. Without pollination, the majority of these plants will produce flowers, but the flowers won't develop into fruit. Others, such as tomatoes, are self-pollinating, but the yield of many varieties of tomatoes is greatly increased if the plants are also pollinated by insects.

HOW TO HELP POLLINATORS

How can you help pollinators? An RHS study of insects visiting garden plants in the UK found that the best way to attract pollinators to your garden is to grow a mix of native, northern hemisphere, and southern hemisphere plants.

Go for variety

Pollinators are attracted to different shapes of flowers, so it makes sense to choose a range of sizes and shapes. Scientists are still researching why certain plants are more attractive to insects. Hoverflies tend to prefer flat, open flowers, such as angelica, sea holly, and fennel, where the nectar and pollen are easy to access. Some members of the daisy family are also magnets

for pollinators. Plants with tubular flowers, such as foxgloves and columbine, are more likely to be visited by insects with a long proboscis, such as butterflies, moths, and some bumblebees. In the vegetable garden, attract pollinators with the flowers of borage, chives, marjoram, mint, rosemary, and sage. Experiment to see which flowers are most popular in your own garden.

A place in the sun

Most flowers prefer sunny conditions, and pollinators, especially butterflies, prefer flowers in sunny spots. This is partly because sunshine can affect nectar production and also perhaps because insects don't need to expend as much energy in warm conditions.

Choose plants that together give a long flowering season, maximizing the period when nectar and pollen are available. Try to provide nectar and pollen all year round, but especially from February to October, when pollinators are most active. If you have room, plant flowering trees such as willow and hazel for early pollen for bees. Trees can make very efficient foraging ground for pollinators, as they provide masses of blooms in a confined area. Flowering exotic plants are useful for the end of the summer.

You can extend the flowering season by deadheading blooms regularly. Alternatively, once plants have flowered early in the season, you can chop them down to revitalize their growth and encourage a second flowering season. Check which plants benefit from this treatment.

A multistory hotel for insects made using natural materials will provide shelter for all sorts of mini beasts. Use dead wood, leaves, loose bark, and hollow stems to fill it.

Bees, butterflies, and many other insects are drawn to open flowers, such as these asters, where the nectar and pollen are easily accessible.

A safe haven

Provide places for insects to shelter, such as patches of long grass left unmowed, favored by many species of moths and some bumblebees. Leave dead stems standing over winter, where insects can take up residence. You can also make or buy an insect hotel, in which various pollinators and other invertebrates can overwinter. Solitary bees like to nest in hollow plant stems. Make them bespoke nests by cutting hollow stems or bamboo canes about ½–¾in (1.5–2cm) diameter into pieces 4–8in (10–20cm) long, and tying them in bundles. Hang these in a sunny, sheltered spot about 5ft (1.5m) above the ground.

Pollinators need water to drink. A shallow dish, with a few stones or twigs to act as perches, is ideal. Alternatively, if you have space, build a wildlife pond (see pp.56–57). Avoid using pesticides in your garden (see pp.50–51), and never spray open flowers that might be visited by pollinators.

Invisible colors

It pays to include a range of hues in your garden because certain colors, while pleasing to us, are less appealing to some pollinators. Studies have found that red, for instance, is generally less attractive to insects. Bees—and most insects with good vision—see better in the blue spectrum and beyond, into the ultraviolet (UV) range. Many flowers have UV markings on them, which are invisible to humans, such as these spirea 'Grefsheim' flowers (below), and these make their colors appear very different to insects. Scientists think these markings act like landing strips, guiding pollinators to nectar and pollen.

CREATE A WILDFLOWER MEADOW

Meadows full of different kinds of flowers and grasses are home to, and feeding grounds for, many different kinds of insects. These insects, in turn, provide food for birds and small mammals. Wildflower meadows have disappeared from much of the countryside, but you can help to revive these habitats by planting a mini-meadow in your own green space. You don't have to have a large country garden to create a meadow: even wildflowers in containers or a small patch is worth cultivating.

A meadow in your garden

If you have space for a perennial meadow in your garden, frame it with mowed grass, or allow it to become an informal boundary between different parts of the garden. You can sow your meadow on a piece of bare ground, or, for a speedier option, lay pregrown wildflower turf.

Both methods will work better if the soil has not been fertilized as wildflowers do best on poor soils, so you may need to strip off the top layer of soil before you start. The secret of success is clean soil, with no perennial weeds or grass that could swamp the annuals—sow yellow rattle to suppress the growth of grasses.

Meadow mixes, such as this mixed native and non-native annual meadow, are packed with different species of flowers and grasses that are alive with busily working insects all summer.

Once your meadow becomes established, you can look forward to insects flitting among the waving grasses and wildflowers every summer.

Grow in containers

Consider growing brightly colored annual wildflowers in containers in sunny spots. Once the plants have finished flowering, leave the stems in the soil to provide winter quarters for

insects and other wildlife. Then clear the soil of stems for sowing a new "meadow" in the following spring.

Growing annual wildflowers in containers allows you to experiment with new colors and flowers every year—some seed mixes contain flowers of the traditional cornfield, while others include jewellike blooms from different parts of the world. Change the plantings annually.

YELLOW RATTLE
(*Rhinanthus minor*)

YOUR WILDFLOWER MEADOW

Follow these steps to make a perennial meadow in your garden.

- Site your meadow in an open and sunny location.

- Clear the ground of perennial weeds such as nettles, docks, and thistles for sowing either in early fall or spring.

- If the soil has been fertilized, scrape off the top 6–8in (15–20cm) before raking the soil to make a fine surface for the seeds.

- Choose a mix that will suit your soil type and aspect.

- Follow the instructions on the seed packet and roll or tread the ground to settle the seeds into the soil.

- If the weather is very dry, water lightly at sowing time. After that, the meadow should not need watering.

- In the first year, cut the meadow when it reaches 4–6in (10–15cm) high. Take away the cuttings so they don't make the soil more fertile.

- From the second year on, the meadow will need cutting only after flowering, but you can leave a small section uncut until spring, so that insects can shelter in it over winter.

MAKE A SCENTED NIGHT GARDEN

The garden at night can be a special place—pale-colored flowers and leaves appear to glimmer in the fading light, and scented plants waft their fragrance intoxicatingly in the air. Some plants, such as evening primrose, are pollinated by crepuscular or nocturnal insects, especially moths, and only open their flowers as it gets dark. The delicately scented flowers of evening primrose visibly open at dusk and seem to glow as the light fades. Others, such as star jasmine and dame's violet, have flowers that are open during the day and at night—they boost their chances of being pollinated by also producing fragrance at night.

Make your outside space a scented haven for sitting in after dark and providing food for pollinating moths, which will take nectar from the flowers. Scented climbers, such as honeysuckle, or annuals, such as tobacco plant and night-scented stock, in pots or borders in sheltered parts of the garden will work well.

The presence of moths will make your garden more biodiverse, too, as both the adults and caterpillars are key food sources for a variety of wildlife including bats, birds, frogs, toads, lizards, hedgehogs, and spiders.

A helping hand for moths

Grow nectar-rich flowers to attract pollinating moths to your garden—such as this convolvulus hawkmoth (right) feeding on the tubular flowers of a tobacco plant—and leave areas of long grass and plant stems for moths to shelter in. Some plants will also provide food for moth caterpillars, and if you have room for a tree, species such as oak, birch, willow, hornbeam, and hawthorn are particularly recommended. Bringing more wildlife into the garden will help to keep a natural balance, reducing pest outbreaks. Gardens that have plenty of moths are good feeding grounds for birds, bats, and other wildlife.

1

2

3

4

5

IN THE NIGHT GARDEN

Choose plants that are most fragrant at night or that open only at dusk to attract nighttime pollinators.

1 Common honeysuckle (*Lonicera periclymenum*) is strongly fragrant in the evening, when the flowers attract pollinating moths.

2 Dame's violet (*Hesperis matronalis*) has purple, cream, or white flowers that are more intensely scented at night.

3 Night-scented stock (*Matthiola longipetala* subsp. *bicornis*) bears white, purple, or pink flowers that are strongly fragrant at night.

4 Night-scented phlox (*Zaluzianskya ovata*) has white flowers with crimson-red backs that are highly scented at night.

5 Night-flowering catchfly (*Silene noctiflora*) opens its flowers only after dusk and attracts pollinating moths.

From summer to early fall, the fragrant yellow flowers of the common evening primrose open in the evening and remain open until late morning.

Is your garden really "green"?

By becoming a more sustainable gardener, you will help your local environment, wildlife, the planet—and yourself.

The way you garden has a huge impact on the environment, both local and globally, and whether that impact is good or bad depends entirely upon the choices you make. The type of compost you buy, the machinery you use, the pots, fertilizers, even the plants you grow can all be detrimental if they're not eco-friendly. How do you know what's "green" and what isn't? The "reduce, reuse, recycle, and reinvest" mantra is a good place to start, but every action that reduces direct or indirect emissions of greenhouse gases can contribute to a healthier planet.

"GREEN" GARDENING

About 500 million plastic plant pots and seed trays are sold in the UK every year. Most end up in landfills, where scientists estimate they take hundreds of years to decompose, but some are burned. Both disposal methods release toxins, including cancer-causing substances, that end up in soil and eventually in groundwater, as well as harmful chemicals and greenhouse gases into the atmosphere. Most plastic production also relies on nonrenewable, oil-based petrochemicals that also contribute to pollution and a changing climate. Recycling pots cuts down on single-use plastic, but the recycling process usually requires some virgin plastic, as well as energy, to make next-generation products.

You can reuse the plastic pots you already have for decades—just be sure to clean them well between uses—and if you have more than you need, offer them to other gardeners. The most sustainable alternative, however, is to avoid plastic altogether. Clay pots and "found" containers such as metal tubs or wooden barrels are better options. You can also buy and grow plants in biodegradable pots, such as rice husk, bamboo, or wood pulp. Many of these can be planted straight into the ground, reducing root disturbance, while others can be broken up and put on the compost heap to decompose.

Home composting can save **772lb (350kg)** of **greenhouse gas emissions** a year by not sending **green waste** to **landfills**.

In **landfills**, **nitrogen-rich** fruit and vegetable peelings release **harmful methane** into the **atmosphere**. But they **compost** into a **balanced fertilizer** when added to **carbon-rich** garden **leaves, twigs, and stems**.

Why composting is crucial

Composting should be at the heart of any green garden. In oxygen-deprived landfill conditions, green waste releases methane, a greenhouse gas that is 28 times more harmful than carbon dioxide. By composting organic matter—lawn and plant clippings, leaves, and kitchen peelings—in aerated heaps, you not only create nutrient-rich compost to enhance your soil's health and structure, but you're also reducing landfill space and eliminating transportation needed to take the waste away. Homemade compost also helps soil retain moisture, which reduces the amount of watering required. Depending on how much compost you make, it can be used as fertilizer, mulch, or as a top dressing—it is also relatively easy to achieve (see pp.204–205). Even the smallest urban patio garden can house a compost bin or a specialized "hot bin," which can also deal with certain types of cooked food waste (see p.205).

You can limit greenhouse gas emissions even further by swapping gas-powered mowers and tools for solar-charged electric ones, including those powered by rechargeable batteries. A push mower is more sustainable than a riding mower, for instance.

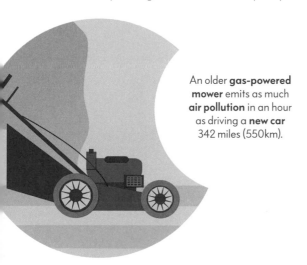

An older **gas-powered mower** emits as much **air pollution** in an hour as driving a **new car** 342 miles (550km).

Opting out of peat

Removing peat from bogs to make compost damages wildlife and the wider environment. As well as being a rare and vital habitat created over thousands of years, peat bogs serve as "carbon sinks," trapping vast amounts of compressed plant material which, if dried, releases carbon dioxide into the atmosphere that accelerates a changing climate. So avoid peat, and use peat-free alternatives instead.

MAKE YOUR OWN COMPOST

Besides helping the planet at large, a compost heap or bin provides a handy place to put plant clippings, stems and grass cuttings, kitchen waste such as fruit and vegetable peels and scraps, and even cardboard and waste paper. More importantly, it's beneficial to life-forms large and small, promoting the biodiversity that, in turn, allows your garden to thrive.

Tiny workers

Composting relies on the action of billions of microorganisms such as bacteria and fungi, and soil creatures such as nematodes, beetles, and worms. Given the right conditions, they break down the compost bin contents, turning them into a dark-brown material with a crumbly, texture like soil. This returns the nutrients from plant matter to the soil whenever you spread it as a mulch or dig it in as a soil conditioner. You can also use it as the basis for making your own potting compost.

Choose a level spot for your bin or heap. Place it on soil to allow the contents to drain and provide access for soil creatures, such as worms. Position it in shade or partial sun, but avoid temperature extremes. If you've only a hard surface like a patio, add a spadeful of soil to the bottom, or a handful of worms to get it started.

It's all about balance

Whether you have an open compost heap or an enclosed bin, the key to composting success is getting the right balance of greens, browns, water, air, and microbes. You need a mixture of about a quarter to a half of green material. Green material includes nitrogen-rich grass clippings, leafy plant matter, and fruit and vegetable peelings. Brown material includes carbon-rich dry leaves, dried twigs, shredded paper, and cardboard (see opposite). Chopping up brown waste will help speed up the composting process.

If your compost turns slimy and smelly, it's usually because it's too wet, which means you have an excess of green material and not enough brown stuff. If you're adding ingredients gradually, build it up in layers, with a moist green layer followed by a dry brown one, and so on.

Keep it moist but airy

Provide enough air and water for the microorganisms in your compost to survive. If your heap is too wet or stodgy, turn it from time to time to loosen the materials and keep them well mixed. Covering the compost, either with a custom-built lid or something like a carpet remnant, will help to raise the temperature, which speeds up the composting process. Your compost should be mature enough to use any time from about six months onward.

> **Home composting** can **divert** up to **331lb (150kg) of food waste** per household per year from local **collection authorities**

GREENS (NITROGEN RICH)

- Grass clippings and some pet bedding
- Soft, leafy plants including annual, noninvasive weeds
- Fruit and vegetable peelings, nonplastic tea bags

BROWNS (CARBON RICH)

- Woody prunings, twigs, dead leaves, straw, wood chippings
- Shredded paper, newspaper, cardboard, vacuum-cleaner contents

NEVER COMPOST

- Bread, meat, or dairy products
- Cooking oil
- Diseased or infested plants
- Plants treated with herbicides or pesticides
- Coated/glossy paper
- Carnivorous animal feces or cat litter

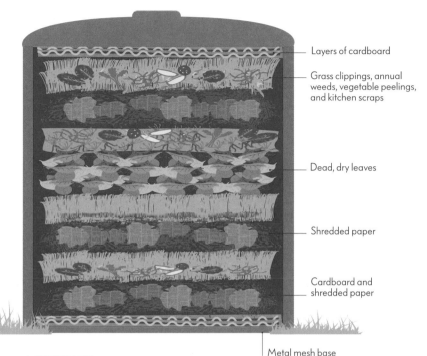

Layers of cardboard

Grass clippings, annual weeds, vegetable peelings, and kitchen scraps

Dead, dry leaves

Shredded paper

Cardboard and shredded paper

Metal mesh base

A GOOD MIX

A good balance of materials is between 25 and 50 percent of green material, and between 75 and 50 percent brown. Keep layers well mixed for aeration. Cover your bin to raise the temperature of the compost, and add a base of metal mesh to keep out rats.

Solutions for small spaces

You can compost in a small space by using a hot bin or wormery. Hot bins are insulated boxes in which temperatures reach 140°F (60°C) or more. This speeds up the composting process (the compost is ready in 30 to 90 days), kills pathogens, and allows some cooked food waste to be used as well as more types of raw food. Wood chips help aerate the contents, and shredded paper balances moisture levels.

Wormeries rely on special worms that decompose chopped-up kitchen waste and small amounts of garden waste. The worms are most active at temperatures between 64 and 77°F (18 and 25°C). The liquid that forms can be drained off, diluted, and used as plant food.

Saving air miles on cut flowers

Many cut flowers travel vast distances to reach us. By buying homegrown or growing all we can at home, we can reduce their impact—and our carbon footprint.

Cultivating your own fruits and vegetables is a no-brainer when it comes to cutting down on food air miles, but what about flowers that adorn our homes? Those blooms were probably grown thousands of miles away, then flown and shipped in, with inevitable environmental consequences. Buy US-grown cut flowers or plant cut-flower plants alongside food crops, however, and you can enjoy botanical beauty while treading more lightly on the earth.

REDUCING THE COST OF HORTICULTURE

From avocados to zinnias, what we purchase has an environmental impact in a variety of ways. Many plants and flowers are grown in other countries, then flown thousands of miles to their destinations, pumping out massive amounts of pollution en route. Around 45 percent of cut flowers sold worldwide are exported from Colombia, Kenya, Ecuador, and Ethiopia to markets in the US, Europe, and Asia. While that figure is lower for ornamental plants, these are also still mostly exported, notably from the Netherlands and Central America. Exporting plants also increases the risk of spreading pests and diseases like ash dieback, sudden oak death, and the bacterium *Xylella*, which can cause disease in more than 350 different types of garden plants and may also affect native plants.

Some commercial growers are addressing the environmental issues in the horticultural industry, including water and chemical overuse, and waste management. When buying cut flowers, choose blooms grown in the US, and seek out the increasing number of retailers that are actively promoting sustainable practices.

Colombia and Ecuador are the world's second- and third-largest **exporters** of **cut flowers**, after the **Netherlands**. More than **15,000 tons (13,600 tonnes)** of **flowers** fly out from **Colombia** and **Ecuador** to the **US** in the three weeks prior to **Valentine's Day**.

Estimated **carbon dioxide emissions** from a flight from **Kenya** to the **Netherlands** are **8,380lb (3,800kg)** and would require **80 tree seedlings** being planted and grown for **10 years** to **offset** the **atmospheric pollution** they cause.

The equivalent of **60 cargo jets** every day deliver **flowers** to the **US** from **Colombia** and **Ecuador** in the three weeks before **Valentine's Day.** They burn around **25 million gallons (114 million litres)** of **fuel**, and release **397,000 tons (360,000 tonnes)** of **carbon dioxide.**

The true price of saying "I love you"

Our desire for particular plants at all times of the year has a massive environmental impact. Consider, for example, the rose: the "flower of love." While Valentine's Day sees a spike in the global demand for roses, vast amounts are flown across the globe all year. The climate in Kenya in East Africa and in Colombia in Latin America are ideal for rose cultivation, and while the low-tech methods used in these countries may have less immediate impact on the environment than those produced under glass closer to home, flying roses halfway around the world contributes to global pollution. Most Kenyan roses are sent to Amsterdam, then distributed to the rest of Europe by road and sea, adding even more to their carbon footprint. By growing flowers in your garden or buying homegrown flowers, you can help to reduce the impact on the environment.

Roses travel approximately **4,150 miles (6,680km)** from **Kenya** to **Amsterdam** in the Netherlands, and **2,485 miles (4,000km)** from **Colombia** to **Miami** to reach the main **cut-flower** wholesalers.

PLANT A YEAR-ROUND CUTTING GARDEN

Choose species for cut flowers that suit your climate and soil type, and select plants that fit the site, whether it is sunny, shady, or in between. Most cut flowers prefer sheltered, sunny spots and moist, free-draining soil, but spring bulbs and some shrubs thrive in partial shade. Enrich the soil with organic matter a few weeks before planting in spring, or in fall for clay soils.

Flowering plot or floral boundary?

The choice is yours: create a bed exclusively for cut flowers and grow them in rows, like vegetables, or weave groups of perennials into existing borders to cut when needed. Space cut-flower plants far enough apart to allow easy access to the blooms. Also consider

PARROT TULIP
(*Tulipa* 'Texas Flame')
Spring-flowering bulb

SUNFLOWER
(*Helianthus annuus*)
Annual that flowers
in summer

SWEET PEA
(*Lathyrus odoratus*)
Annual that flowers
in summer

DAFFODIL
(*Narcissus*)
Spring-flowering bulb

planting boundaries and borders with shrubs and trees that offer spring blossom, berries, and evergreen foliage to vary your decorative choices.

Grow with the seasons in mind

Plant for all seasons and pick a range of flowers, leaves, stems, berries, and seedheads to decorate your home every month of the year. Evergreen foliage and colorful stems in winter can be just as attractive as a bunch of fresh blooms in spring.

Plant spring bulbs in fall to kickstart the new year's displays with colorful flowers. Sow annuals such as snapdragons, sunflowers, and cosmos in spring in pots or trays inside, then move young plants outside after the last frosts. Plant them between the faded leaves of the spring bulbs to maximize your space.

Dahlias and tender bulbs planted in spring offer a long season of flowers. In cold areas, lift tubers and bulbs once the leaves have been blackened by frost and store them indoors for the winter.

Perennials such as sea holly and penstemon flower year after year, and will thrive if mulched with a layer of organic matter, such as well-rotted garden compost, applied on top of the soil in spring.

DAHLIA
(*Dahlia* 'Carolina Wagemans')
Perennial that flowers from summer to fall

HONESTY
(*Lunaria annua*)
Hardy annual with seed pods in fall

LOVE-IN-A-MIST
(*Nigella damascena* 'Miss Jekyll Blue')
Annual that flowers in summer

ALLIUM
(*Allium hollandicum* 'Purple Sensation')
Spring-flowering bulb with seedheads in late summer

A FROSTY CANVAS
In Dutch landscape designer Piet Oudorf's perennial garden for the Hauser & Wirth gallery and arts center, the strong forms of *Echinacea pallida* seedheads are left to create winter interest among the grasses and to provide shelter for insects.

INDEX

Page numbers in *italics* refer to illustrations.

REFERENCES

Plants as potential pollution-busters

Abhijith et al. (2017). "Air pollution abatement performances of green infrastructure in open road and built-up street canyon environments—a review". *Atmospheric Environment*, 162: 71–86.

Blanuša, T. Royal Horticultural Society, ongoing research

Blanuša, T., Garratt, M., Cathcart-James, M., Hunt, L., and Cameron, R. W. F. (2019). "Urban hedges: a review of plant species and cultivars for ecosystem service delivery in northwest Europe." *Urban Forestry & Urban Greening*, 44. 126391.

Blevin, R. (2019). "Plant hedges to combat near-road pollution exposure". University of Surrey. www.surrey.ac.uk/news/plant-hedges-combat-near-road-pollution-exposure

Dover, J., Phillips, S. (2015). "Particulate Pollution Capture by Green Screens along the A38 Bristol Street in Birmingham." The Green Wall Centre, Staffordshire University. Final Report, vol. 3 16-11–15. www.staffs.ac.uk/research/greenwall

Dzierżanowski, K., Popek, R., Gawrońska, H., Sæbø, A., and Gawroński, S.W. (2011). "Deposition of Particulate Matter of Different Size Fractions on Leaf Surfaces and in Waxes of Urban Forest Species". *International Journal of Phytoremediation*, 13:10, 1037–1046.

Ferranti, E.J.S., MacKenzie, A.R., Levine, J.G., Ashworth, K and Hewitt, C.N. (2019) "First Steps in Air Quality for Built Environment Practitioners". Technical Report. University of Birmingham & TDAG. (Unpublished)

Janhäll, S. (2015). "Review on urban vegetation and particle air pollution—Deposition and dispersion". Swedish National Road and Transport Research Institute-VTI, Sweden. *Atmospheric Environment*, 105: 130–137.

Office for National Statistics. (2018). "UK air pollution removal: how much pollution does vegetation remove in your area?" www.ons.gov.uk/economy/environmentalaccounts/articlesukairpollutionremovalhowmuchpollutiondoesvegetationremoveinyourarea/2018-07-30

Royal College of Physicians. "Every breath we take: the lifelong impact of air pollution". (2016). London: RCP. www.rcplondon.ac.uk/projects/outputs/every-breath-we-take-lifelong-impact-air-pollution

Royal Horticultural Society. "Hedges: selection". www.rhs.org.uk/advice/profile?PID=351

Sæbø, A., Popek, R., Nawrot, B., Hanslin, H.M., Gawronska, H., and Gawronski, S.W. (2012). "Plant species differences in particulate matter accumulation on leaf surfaces". *Sci Total Environ*, 15: 427–428: 347–54.

Stubley, P. (2018) "First evidence of soot air pollution reaching the placenta found in London mothers, new study says". www.independent.co.uk/news/health/air-pollution-pregnant-women-london-study-placenta-first-evidence-a8539861.html.

The Tree Council. "Urban Hedges Reduce the Impact of Air Pollution". www.treecouncil.org.uk/Press-News/Hedges-reduce-the-impact-of-air-pollution.

Townsend, M. (2018). "What is air pollution and what can I do to help?". Woodland Trust. www.woodlandtrust.org.uk/blog/2018/05/air-pollution/

Weerakkody et al. (2018). "Evaluating the impact of individual leaf traits on atmospheric particulate matter accumulation using natural and synthetic leaves". The Green Wall Centre, Staffordshire University. *Urban Foresty & Urban Greening*, 30: 98–107.

Plants as potential sound-proofing

Azkorra, Z., Pérez, G., Coma, J., Cabeza, L.F., Bures, S. Álvaro, J.E., Erkoreka, A., and Urrestarazu, M. (2015). "Evaluation of green walls as a passive acoustic insulation system for buildings". *Applied Acoustics*, 89: 46–56.

Calarco, F.M.A. (2015). "Soundscape design of water features used in outdoor spaces where road traffic noise is audible". School of Energy, Geoscience, Infrastructure and Society, 59, 65.

Dobson, M., Ryan, J. (2000). "Trees and shrubs for noise control". Arboricultural Advisory and Information Service, APN 6.

Dr. Patrick Osborne, Reader in Applied Ecology, Director of Programmes for Environmental Science, University of Southampton—consultation on sound.

Yang, F., Bao, Z., Zhujun, Z., and Liu, J. (2010). "The Investigation of Noise Attenuation by Plants and the Corresponding Noise-Reducing Spectrum". *Journal of Environmental Health*, 72(8):8–15.

Creating a low-allergen garden

2010 RHS Chelsea Flower Show garden, University of Worcester Garden by Olivia Kirk. www.oliviakirkgardens.com/university-of-worcester.php

www.allergicliving.com/2013/03/14/low-allergy-plants/

www.allergyuk.org/information-and-advice/statistics

Nex, S. "Not to Be Sniffed at". www.rhs.org.uk/about-the-rhs/publications/the-garden/2018-issues/march/allergen-planting-not-to-be-sniffed-at.pdf

Sedghy, F., Varasteh, A., Sankian, M., and Moghadam, M. (2018). "Interaction Between Air Pollutants and Pollen Grains: The Role on the Rising Trend in Allergy". *Rep Biochem Mol Biol*, 6(2): 219–224. www.ncbi.nlm.nih.gov/pmc/articles/PMC5941124/

Managing pests the natural way

www.defenders.co.uk/about-defenders/about-defenders.html

Flowerdew, B. (2000). *Bob Flowerdew's Complete Book of Companion Gardening*. Kyle Cathie.

www.greengardener.co.uk

Gilliom, R.J., Hamilton, P.A. "Pesticides in the Nation's Streams and Ground Water, 1992–2001—A Summary". (2006). USGS.

Helyer, N., Brown, K., Cattlin, N.D. (2014). *Biological Control in Plant Protection*.

Parker, J.E., Snyder, W.E., Hamilton, G.C., and Rodriguez-Saona, C. (2014). "Companion Planting and Insect Pest Control". IntechOpen. www.intechopen.com/books/weed-and-pest-control-conventional-and-new-challenges/companion-planting-and-insect-pest-control

http://press.rhs.org.uk/RHS-Science-and-Advice/Press-releases/RHS-slug-study-busts-home-remedy-myths.aspx

Salisbury, A. RHS principal entomologist—consultation on companion planting.

Water Science School. "Pesticides in Groundwater". USGS. www.usgs.gov/special-topic/water-science-school/science/pesticides-groundwater?qt-science_center_objects=0#qt-science_center_objects

Feel good with Vitamin G

Hunt, A., Stewart, D., Burt, J. & Dillon, J. (2016). "Monitor of Engagement with the Natural Environment: a pilot to develop an indicator of visits to the natural environment by children". *Natural England Commissioned Reports*, No. 208.

The King's Fund. "Access to green and open spaces and the role of leisure services". Research document citing Groenewegen et al. (2003). www.kingsfund.org.uk/projects/improving-publics-health/access-green-and-open-spaces-and-role-leisure-services

Kuo, F. E. M. (2013). "Nature-deficit disorder: evidence, dosage, and treatment". *Journal of Policy Research in Tourism, Leisure and Events*, Vol. 5: Issue 2, 172–186.

Soga, M., Gaston, K.J. and Yamaura, Y (2017). "Gardening is beneficial for health: a meta-analysis". *Prev Med Rep*, 5: 92–99.

Ulrich, R. S., Lundén, O., and Eltinge, J L. (1993). "Effects of exposure to nature and abstract pictures on patients recovering from heart surgery". *Psychophysiology*, 30: 7.

How your garden reboots your brain

Clay, R. (2001). "Green is good for you". *American Psychological Association*, vol. 32, no. 4. www.apa.org/monitor/apr01/greengood

Gross, H. (2018). *The Psychology of Gardening*. 1st ed. (The Psychology of Everything). Abingdon: Routledge, pp.58–60

Hůla M., Flegr J. (2016). "What flowers do we like? The influence of shape and color on the rating of flower beauty". *PeerJ*, 4:e2106 https://doi.org/10.7717/peerj.2106

www.urbanplanters.co.uk/benefits-of-plants/

How gardening can boost your self-esteem

Gross, H. (2018). *The Psychology of Gardening*. 1st edn (The Psychology of Everything). Abingdon: Routledge.

Wells, N., Gary Evans, G. (2003) "Nearby Nature". *Environment and Behavior*, 35(3): 311 330. www.researchgate.net/publication/246924740_Nearby_Nature

Gardening to overcome isolation

Pantell, M., Rehkopf, D., Jutte, D., Syme, L., Balmes, J., and Adler, N. (2013). "Social Isolation: A Predictor of Mortality Comparable to Traditional Clinical Risk Factors". *Am J Public Health*, 11: 2056–2062.

Wood, C.J., Pretty, J., Griffin, M. (2016). "A case-control study of the health and well-being benefits of allotment gardening". *Journal of Public Health*, vol. 38, issue 3, 336–344. https://academic.oup.com/jpubhealth/article/38/3/e336/2239844

Yang, Y.C., McClintock, M.K., Kozloski, M. and Ting Li, T. (2013) "Social Isolation and Adult Mortality". *Journal of Health and Social Behaviour*.

The powerful impact of scent

Hyunju, J., Rodiek, S., Fujii, E., Miyazaki, Y., Bum-Jin, P. 4 and Seoung-Won, A. (2013). "Physiological and Psychological Response to Floral Scent". *Hort. Science*, vol. 48: issue 1: 82–88. https://journals.ashs.org/hortsci/view/journals/hortsci/48/1/article-p82.xml

Moss, M., Cook, J., Wesnes, K., Duckett, P. (2003). "Aromas of rosemary and lavender essential oils differentially affect cognition and mood in healthy adults". *Intern. J. Neuroscience*, 113:15–38. https://inchemistry.acs.org/content/inchemistry/en/atomic-news/summer-scents.html

Wood-Black, F. (2017). "How Scent Chemicals in Flowers Perfume the Summer Air". ACS. https://inchemistry.acs.org/content/inchemistry/en/atomic-news/summer-scents.html

Harnessing the power of color

Elsadek, M., Sayak, S., Fujii, E., Koriesh, E., Moghazy, E., and El Fatah, Y.A. (2013). "Human emotional and psycho-physiological responses to plant color stimuli". *Journal of Food, Agriculture and Environment*, 11: 1584–1591.

Palmer, S.E., Karen B. Schloss, K.B. and Kay, P. (2010). "An ecological valence theory of human color preference". *Proceedings of the National Academy of Sciences of the United States of America*, vol. 107, 19: 8877–8882.

Wilms, L., Oberfled, D. (2018). "Color and emotion: effects of hue, saturation, and brightness". *Psychol Res*, 82(5): 896–914.

The restorative effects of water

Gascon, M., Zijlema, W., Vert, C., White, M.P., Nieuwenhuijsen, M.J. (2017). "Outdoor blue spaces, human health and well-being: A systematic review of quantitative studies". *Int J Hyg Environ Health*, 220(8): 1207–1221.

Griffiths, A. RHS.

White, M.P., Alcock, I., Wheeler, B.W., Depledge, M.H. (2013). "Coastal proximity, health and well-being: Results from a longitudinal panel survey". *Health & Place*, vol. 23. 97–103.

The positive power of birdsong

Alvarsson et al. (2010). "Stress Recovery during Exposure to Nature Sound and Environmental Noise". *International Journal of Environmental Research and Public Health*, 7, 1036–1046.

British Trust for Ornithology. (2019). "Boom time at Britain's bird feeders". *Nature Communications*. www.bto.org/press-releases/boom-time-britains-bird-feeders

British Trust for Ornithology. "Plants for fruits and seeds". www.bto.org/our-science/projects/gbw/gardens-wildlife/gardening/plants-fruit-seeds

Hedblom, M., Heyman, E., Antonsson, H., and Gunnarsson, B. (2014). "Bird song diversity influences young people's appreciation of urban landscapes". Department of Biological and Environmental Sciences, University of Gothenburg. *Urban Forestry & Urban Greening*, 13: 469–474

Ratcliffe et al. (2016). "Associations with bird sounds: How do they relate to perceived restorative potential?" *Journal of Environmental Psychology*, 47: 136-144

RSPB. "Making and placing a nestbox". www.rspb.org.uk/birds-and-wildlife/advice/how-you-can-help-birds/nestboxes/nestboxes-for-small-birds/making-and-placing-a-bird-box/

Dirt is good for you

Bloomfield, S.F., Rook, G.A.W., Elizabeth, A. Scott, E. A., Shanahan, F., Stanwell-Smith, R., and

Turner, P. (2016) "Time to abandon the hygiene hypothesis: new perspectives on allergic disease, the human microbiome, infectious disease prevention and the role of targeted hygiene". *Perspectives in Public Health*, vol 136, no 4 l. www.grahamrook.net/OldFriends/oldfriends.html

Riedler et al. (2001) "Exposure to farming in early life and development of asthma and allergy: a cross-sectional survey". *Lancet*, 358(9288): 1129–33. www.ncbi.nlm.nih.gov/pubmed/11597666

Schlanger, Z. (2017) "Dirt has a microbiome, and it may double as an antidepressant". https://qz.com/993258/dirt-has-a-microbiome-and-it-may-double-as-an-antidepressant/

Why the garden beats the gym

Guinness, B. (2008). *Garden Your Way to Health and Fitness*, Portland, OR: Timber Press.

Hawkins, J.L., Smith, A., Backx, K., and Clayton, D.A. (2015). "Exercise Intensities of Gardening Tasks Within Older Adult Allotment Gardeners in Wales". Aging and Physical Activity.

Harvard Health Publishing. (Updated 2018.) "Calories burned in 30 minutes for people of three different weights". www.health.harvard.edu/diet-and-weight-loss/calories-burned-in-30-minutes-of-leisure-and-routine-activities

Olafsdottir, G et al. (2016). "Green exercise is associated with better cell aging profiles". *The European Journal of Public Health*, 26. www.researchgate.net/publication/311695511_Green_exercise_is_associated_with_better_cell_aging_profiles

Shippen, J., Alexander, P., and Barbara May, B. (2017). "A Novel Biomechanical Analysis of Horticultural Digging". *HortTechnology*, 27(6).

The secret life of healthy soil

Pimentel, D. (2006) "Soil Erosion: A Food and Environmental Threat". *Environment, Development and Sustainability*, 8: 119. https://doi.org/10.1007/s10668-005-1262-8

Tree, I. (2019). *Wilding: The return of nature to a British farm*, London: Pan Macmillan.

Van Groenigen, J.W., Lubbers, I.M., Vos, H.M.J., Brown, G.G., De Deyn, G.B. and van Groenigen, K.J. (2014). "Earthworms increase plant production: A meta-analysis". *Scientific Reports*. https://www.researchgate.net/publication/265647813_Earthworms_increase_plant_production_A_meta-analysis/download

The detoxing power of plants

Gellerman, B. (2011). "Sunflowers used to clean up radiation". *Japan Today*.

Jiang, Y., Lei, M. Duan, L., Longhurst, P.J. (2015) "Integrating phytoremediation with biomass valorisation and critical element recovery: A UK contaminated land perspective". *Biomass and Energy*, 83: 328–339.

Ojuederie, O.B., Babalola, O.O. (2017). "Microbial and Plant-Assisted Bioremediation of Heavy Metal Polluted Environments: A Review". Researchgate. www.researchgate.net/figure/Processes-used-in-phytoremediation-of-heavy-metals-Figure-designed-not-cited_fig1_321781831

Science Communication Unit, University of the West of England, Bristol (2013). "Science for Environment Policy In-depth Report: Soil Contamination: Impacts on Human Health". Report produced for the European Commission DG Environment. http://ec.europa.eu/science-environment-policy

University of Eastern Finland. (2014). "Willow trees are cost-efficient cleaners of contaminated soil." *ScienceDaily*.

A medicine chest in the garden

Petrovska, B.B. (2012). "Historical review of medicinal plants' usage". *Pharmacogn Rev*, 6(11): 1–5. www.ncbi.nlm.nih.gov/pmc/articles/PMC3358962/

The Royal College of Physicians' Garden of Medicinal Plants at https://garden.rcplondon.ac.uk/

www-tc.pbs.org/wgbh/nova/julian/media/lrk-disp-plantmedicines.pdf

Growing your own food

Abuajah, C. A., Ogbonna, A.C., and Osuji, C. M. "Functional components and medicinal properties of food: a review". www.ncbi.nlm.nih.gov/pmc/articles/PMC4397330/

Porter, Y. (2012). "Antioxidant properties of green broccoli and purple-sprouting broccoli under different cooking conditions". *Bioscience Horizons*, vol. 5.

Tree, I. (2019). *Wilding: The return of nature to a British farm*, London: Pan Macmillan, pp.280–281.

Wong, J. (2017). *How to eat better*. London: Mitchell Beazley.

The cooling effect of plants

Armson, D., Rahman, M.A., Ennos, A.R. (2013). "A comparison of the shading effectiveness of five different street tree species in Manchester, UK". *Arboriculture & Urban Forestry*, 39 (4): 157–164.

"Benefits of a living wall". www.sempergreen.com/en/solutions/living-wall/living-wall-benefits

Brown and Gillespie. (1995). "Leaf Absorption, Transmission and Reflection of Solar Radiation". https://www.researchgate.net/figure/Leaf-Absorption-Transmission-and-Reflection-of-Solar-Radiation-Source-Brown-and_fig2_224054095

Cameron et al. (2015). "A *Hedera* green façade—Energy performance and saving under different maritime-temperate, winter weather conditions". *Building and Environment*, 92: 111–121.

Coutts, A. "Green infrastructure for cities". Monash University, Melbourne. http://www.meteo.fr/icuc9/presentations/PLENARY/PLENARY4.pdf

Enos, R. "Can trees really cool our cities down?". (2015). *The Conversation*. http://theconversation.com/can-trees-really-cool-our-cities-down-44099

Dunnett, N., Kingsbury, N. (2008). *Planting Green Roofs and Living Walls*, London: Timber Press.

Grant, G., Gedge, D. "Living Roofs and Walls from policy to practice". https://livingroofs.org/wp-content/uploads/2019/04/LONDON-LIVING-ROOFS-WALLS-REPORT-2019.pdf

"Greener cities". www.vertiss.net/en/green-wall/benefits/insulation

Liu, K.K.Y. "Energy efficiency and environmental benefits of rooftop gardens". (2002). *Construction Canada*, vol. 44: no. 2, 17, 20–23.

Monteiro, M.V., Blanuša, T. (2015). "The Cooling Effects of Green Roofs". *The Plantsman*.

Monteiro, M.V., Blanuša, T., Hadley, P., Cameron, R.W.F. (2016). "Implication of plant selection for building insulation". *Acta horticulturae*, 1108: 339–344.

Monteiro, M.V., Blanuša, T., Verhoef, A., Richardson, M., Hadley, P. and Cameron, R. W. F. (2017) "Functional green roofs: importance of plant choice in maximizing summertime environmental cooling and substrate insulation potential". *Energy and Buildings*, 141: 56–68.

Perez et al. "Vertical Greenery Systems for energy saving in buildings: a review". *Renewable and Sustainable Energy Reviews*, 39 (2014) 139–165.

Perini et al. "Greening the building envelope, façade greening and living wall systems". (2011). *Open Journal of Ecology*, vol.1, no.1, 1–8.

Perini et al. "Vertical greening systems and the effect on air flow and temperature on the building envelope". (2011). *Building and Environment*, 46: 2287–2294.

RHS. "Trees near buildings". www.rhs.org.uk/advice/profile?pid=225

Save energy with plants

Giometto, M.G., Christen, A., Egli, P.E., Schmid, M.F., Tooke, R.T., Coops, N.C., and Parlange, M.B. (2017). "Effects of trees on mean wind, turbulence and momentum exchange within and above a real urban environment". www.sciencedirect.com/science/article/pii/S0309170817306486

"Greener Cities". www.vertiss.net/en/green-wall/benefits/insulation

Liu, Y. and Harris, D.J. (2008). "Effects of shelterbelt trees on reducing heating-energy consumption of office buildings in Scotland". *Applied Energy*, Elsevier. 85(2–3): 115–127.

Perez et al. (2014). "Vertical Greenery Systems for energy saving in buildings: a review". *Renewable and Sustainable Energy Reviews*, 39: 139–165.

Future-proofing for drought

Allen, M.R. et al. (2018): "Global Warming of 1.5°C". An IPCC Special Report on the impacts of global warming.

Cameron, Blanuša et al (2012). "The domestic garden—its contribution to urban green infrastructure". *Urban Forestry & Urban Greening*, 11: 129–137.

Cross, R. and Spencer, R. (2009). "Sustainable Gardens". Clayton, Vic: CSIRO Publishing.

European Environment Agency. (2018). "Water Use in Europe—Quantity and Quality Face Big Challenges".

Midgley, S., Steyn, W., and Schmeisser, M. (2018). "What you need to know about orchard water use". Hortgro Science. *Fresh Quarterly*.

RHS. "Gardening in a Changing Climate". www.rhs.org.uk/climate-change

RHS. "Lawns: care during drought". www.rhs.org.uk/Advice/profile?pid=417

RHS. "Water Collecting, Storing and Re-Using". www.rhs.org.uk/advice/profile?pid=313

Richmond, T. "Mulching: Tips for Beginners". *Journal of the American Rhododendron Society*. https://scholar.lib.vt.edu/ejournals/JARS/v46n4/v46n4-richmond.htm

www.waterwise.org.uk

Make your garden a no-flood zone

Adams, C.R. (1998). *Principles of Horticulture, Third Edition*. Butterworth-Heinemann.

Bray, B., Gedge, D., Grant, G., and Leuthvilay, L. "UK Rain Garden Guide". https://raingardens.info/wp-content/uploads/2012/07/UKRainGarden-Guide.pdf

Committee on Climate Change. "UK Climate Change Risk Assessment 2017". www.theccc.org.uk/wp-content/uploads/2016/07/UK-CCRA-2017-Synthesis-Report-Committee-on-Climate-Change.pdf

Environmental Law. "Types of flooding". www.environmentlaw.org.uk/rte.asp?id=100

Federal Interagency Stream Restoration Working Group. "The urban watershed problem".

www.researchgate.net/figure/The-urban-watershed-problem-source-the-Federal-Interagency-Stream-Restoration-Working_fig1_328335823

RHS. Climate Change Report. www.rhs.org.uk/science/gardening-in-a-changing-world/climate-change

RHS. "Rain gardens". www.rhs.org.uk/advice/profile?PID=1009

Sterling, T.M. (2004). "Transpiration—Water Movement through Plants". www.sciencemag.org/site/feature/misc/webfeat/vis2005/show/transpiration.pdf

Tree Canopy BMP. "Stormwater benefits of trees". http://treecanopybmp.org/tree-canopy-bmps/stormwater-benefits-of-trees

Thames Water. "What causes sewer flooding?". www.thameswater.co.uk/help-and-advice/drains-and-sewers/sewer-flooding-who-to-contact/what-causes-sewer-flooding

Plant a haven for pollinators

BBC Future. "What would happen if bees went extinct?" www.bbc.com/future/story/20140502-what-if-bees-went-extinct

Butterfly Conservation. https://butterfly-conservation.org/

Garbuzov. M., Ratnieks, F.L.W. (2013). "Quantifying variation among garden plants in attractiveness to bees and other flower-visiting insects". *Functional Ecology*.

Potts, S.G et al. (2016). "Safeguarding pollinators and their values to human well-being". *Nature*, vol. 540: 220–229.

RHS. "Moth in your garden". www.rhs.org.uk/advice/profile?pid=499

RHS. "Plants for bugs". www.rhs.org.uk/plants4bugs

RHS "Plants for pollinators". www.rhs.org.uk/science/conservation-biodiversity/wildlife/plants-for-pollinators

Salisbury et al. (2015) "Enhancing gardens as habitats for flower-visiting aerial insects (pollinators): should we plant native or exotic species". *Journal of Applied Ecology*. 52: 1156–1164

Is your garden really "green?"

Barretta, G.E., Alexander, P.D., Robinson, J.S., Bragg, N.C. (2016). "Achieving environmentally sustainable growing media for soilless plant cultivation systems—A Review". *Scientia Horticulturae*, 212: 220–234.

Higgins, A. "Is this popular gardening material bad for the planet?" (2017). *Washington Post*. www.washingtonpost.com/lifestyle/home/should-sustainable-gardeners-use-peat-moss/2017/05/09/1fc746f0-3118-11e7-9534-00e4656c22aa_story.html?noredirect=on&utm_term=.7079e88e5d60

Kahy, D. (2019). "For the sake of the climate we must stop believing magical stories about plastics and recycling". Unearthed. https://unearthed.greenpeace.org/2019/07/01/for-the-sake-of-the-climate-we-must-stop-believing-magical-stories-about-plastics-and-recycling/

National Geographic Society Newsroom. (2018). "7 Things You Didn't Know About Plastic (and Recycling)". https://blog.nationalgeographic.org/2018/04/04/7-things-you-didnt-know-about-plastic-and-recycling/

RHS. "Peat-free growing media". www.rhs.org.uk/Advice/Profile?pid=441

www.yousustain.com

Saving air miles on cut flowers

Atmosfair. www.atmosfair.de

Bek, David. "Sustainable Business is Good Business: A view from the Cut Flower Industry". https://blogs.coventry.ac.uk/researchblog/sustainable-business-is-good-business-a-view-from-the-cut-flower-industry/

CBI Product Factsheet: "Fresh Cut Flowers and Foliage in the European unspecialised market".

Central America data. "USA reduces Imports of Flowers and Ornamental Plants". www.centralamericadata.com/en/article/home/USA_Imports_Less_Flowers_and_Ornamental_Plants

Del Valle, G. (2019). "The hidden environmental cost of Valentine's Day roses". *Vox*. www.vox.com/the-goods/2019/2/12/18220984/valentines-day-flowers-roses-environmental-effects

Raboresearch. "World Floriculture Map 2016: Equator Countries Gathering Speed". https://research.rabobank.com/far/en/sectors/regional-food-agri/world_floriculture_map_2016.html

United States Environmental Protection Agency. www.epa.gov/energy/greenhouse-gas-equivalencies-calculator

FURTHER READING

Adevi, A.A. and Mårtensson, F., (2013). "Stress rehabilitation through garden therapy: The garden as a place in the recovery from stress". *Urban Forestry & Urban Greening*, 12(2), 230–237.

Aerts, R., Honnay, O., and Van Nieuwenhuyse, A., (2018). "Biodiversity and human health: mechanisms and evidence of the positive health effects of diversity in nature and green spaces". *British Medical Bulletin*, 127(1), 5–22.

Appleton, J., (1988). "Prospects and refuges revisited". J.L. Nasar (Ed.) *Environmental aesthetics: Theory, research, and applications*, pp. 27–44. Cambridge: Cambridge University Press.

Barton, H. and Grant, M., (2006). "A health map for the local human habitat. *The Journal for the Royal Society for the Promotion of Health*, 126(6), 252–253.

Barton, H., Thompson, S., Burgess, S. And Grant. M., (2017). *The Routledge Handbook of Planning for Well-Being: Shaping a sustainable and healthy future*, 1st ed. London: Routledge.

Beatley, T., (2017). "Biophilic Cities and Healthy Societies". *Urban Planning*, 2(4), 1–4.

Brindley, P.G., Jorgensen, A., and Maheswaran, R. (2018). "Domestic gardens and self-reported health: a national population study". *International Journal of Health Geographics*, 17(31), 1–11.

Buck, D. (2016). *Gardens and health: Implications for policy and practice*. Technical report. London: The King's Fund, commissioned by the National Gardens Scheme.

Cameron, R.W., Blanuša, T., Taylor, J.E., Salisbury, A., Halstead, A.J., et al., (2012). "The domestic garden—Its contribution to urban green infrastructure". *Urban Forestry & Urban Greening*, 11:129–137.

Cameron, R.W., (2014). "Health and well-being". *Horticulture: Plants for People and Places*, Vol. 3. Dordrecht, Springer. pp. 1001–1023.

Cameron, R.W. and Blanuša, T. (2016). "Green infrastructure and ecosystem services—is the devil in the detail?" *Annals of Botany*, 118(3), 377–391.

Cameron, R.W. and Hitchmough, J. (2016). *Environmental Horticulture: Science and Management of Green Landscapes*, London: CABI Publishing.

Clayton, S. (2007). "Domesticated Nature: Motivations for Gardening and Perceptions of Environmental Impact". *Journal of Environmental Psychology*, 27(3), 215–224.

Cooper Marcus, C. and Sachs, N.A. (2013). *Therapeutic Landscapes: An Evidence-Based Approach to Designing Healing Gardens and Restorative Outdoor Spaces*. John Wiley & Sons.

Cox, D.T.C., Shanahan, D.F., Hudson, H.L., Fuller, R.A., Gaston, K.J. (2018). "The impact of urbanisation on nature dose and the implications for human health". *Landscape and Urban Planning*, 179, 72–80.

Davis, J.N., Spaniol, M.R. and Somerset, S., (2015). "Sustenance and sustainability: maximizing the impact of school gardens on health outcomes". *Public health nutrition*, 18(13), 2358–2367.

Dennis, M. and James, P. (2017). "Evaluating the relative influence on population health of domestic gardens and green space along a rural-urban gradient". *Landscape and Urban Planning*, 15, 343–351.

de Vries, S., van Dillen, S.M.E., Groenewegen, P.P., and Spreeuwenberg, P. (2013). "Streetscape greenery and health: stress, social cohesion and physical activity as mediators". *Social Science & Medicine*, 94, 26–33.

Elliot, A.J., Fairchild, M.D. and Franklin, A. ed. (2018). *Handbook of Colour Psychology* (Cambridge Handbooks in Psychology). Cambridge: Cambridge University Press.

Flies, E.J., Skelly, C., Negi, S.S., Prabhakaran, P., Liu, Q., Liu, K., Goldizen, F.C., Lease, C. and Weinstein, P., (2017). "Biodiverse green spaces: a prescription for global urban health". *Frontiers in Ecology and the Environment*, 15(9), 510–516.

Gayle Souter-Brown, (2014). *Landscape and Urban Design for Health and Well-Being: Using Healing, Sensory and Therapeutic Gardens*. Abingdon: Routledge.

Genter, C., Roberts, A., Richardson, J., and Shea, M. (2015). "The contribution of allotment gardening to health and well-being: A systematic review of the literature". *British Journal of Occupational Therapy*, 78(10), 593–605.

Grahn, P. and Stigsdotter, A.U. K. (2010). "The relation between perceived sensory dimensions of urban green space and stress restoration". *Landscape and Urban Planning*, 94(3-4), 264–275.

Gross, H. (2018). *The Psychology of Gardening*. 1st edn (The Psychology of Everything). Abingdon: Routledge.

Hartig, T. and Cooper Marcus, C. (2006). "Healing gardens—places for nature in health care". *The Lancet*, 368, 36–37.

Hartig, T., Mitchell, R., de Vries, S., and Frumkin, H. (2014). "Nature and Health". *Annual Review of Public Health*, 35(1), 207–228.

Hawkins, J. L., Thirlaway, K. J., Backx, K., and Clayton, D. A. (2011). Allotment gardening and other leisure activities for stress reduction and healthy aging. *Hort-Technology*, 21(5), 577–585.

Kamp., D.A. (2016). *Healing Garden*. Mulgrave, Vic.: The Images Publishing Group.

Kaplan, R. and Kaplan, S. (1989). *The experience of nature: a psychological perspective*, Cambridge: Cambridge University Press.

Kellert, S.R. and Wilson, E.O. (1993). *The Biophilia Hypothesis*, Washington, DC: Island Press.

Louv, R. (2005). *Last Child in the Woods: Saving Our Children from Nature-Deficit Disorder*, Chapel Hill, NC: Algonquin Books.

Lovell, R. (2018). "Health and the natural environment: A review of evidence, policy, practice and opportunities for the future". European Center for Environment & Human Health. (Defra Project Code BE0109). Exeter, University of Exeter Medical School.

Qing, Li. (2009). "Effect of forest bathing trips on human immune function". *Environmental Health and Preventive Medicine*, 15(1),9–17.

Royal Horticultural Society, Farrell, Holly. (2017). *Gardening for Mindfulness*. London: Mitchell Beazley.

Soga, M., Gaston, K.J., and Yamaura, Y. (2016). "Gardening is beneficial for health: A meta-analysis". *Preventive Medicine Reports*, 5, 92–99.

Stigsdotter, U.K. and Grahn, P. (2002). "What makes a garden a healing garden?" *Journal of Therapeutic Horticulture*, 60–69.

Ulrich, R. S. (1983). "Aesthetic and Affective Response to Natural Environment". *Behavior and the Natural Environment*, 85–125.

Ulrich, R.S., Simons, R.F., Losito, B.D., Fiorito, E., Miles, M.A., and Zelson, M. (1991). "Stress recovery during exposure to natural and urban environments". *Journal of Environmental Psychology*, 11(3):201–230.

Ulrich, S., Lennartsson., M., et.al., (2014). "Benefits of food growing for health & well-being—overview of the evidence report", Garden Organic and Sustain.

Unruh, A.M., (2002). "The meaning of gardens and gardening in daily life: A comparison between gardeners with serious health problems and healthy participants". *XXVI International Horticultural Congress: Expanding Roles for Horticulture in Improving Human Well-Being and Life Quality*, 639, 67–73.

van Den Berg, A.E. and Custers, M.H.G. (2011). "Gardening promotes neuroendocrine and affective restoration from stress". *Journal of Health Psychology*, 16(1), 3–11.

van Den Berg, M., van Poppel, M., van Kamp, I., Andrusaityte, S., Balseviciene, B., et al. (2016). "Visiting green space is associated with mental health and vitality: A cross-sectional study in four European cities". *Health and Place*, 38,8–15.

van Den Bosch, M. and Bird, W., editors (2018). *Oxford Textbook of Nature and Public Health—The role of nature in improving the health of a population*, Oxford: Oxford University Press.

Von Hertzen, L., Hanski, I. and Haahtela, T. (2011). "Natural immunity. Biodiversity loss and immmflammatory diseases are two global megatrends that might be related". *EMBO reports*, 12(11), 1089–1093.

Wandersee, J.H., & Schussler, E.E., 1999. "Preventing Plant Blindness". *The American Biology Teacher*, 61(2), 82–86.

Ward Thompson, C., Roe, J.J., Aspinall, P., Mitchell, R., Clow, A. and Miller, D. (2012). "More green space is linked to less stress in deprived communities: Evidence from salivary cortisol patterns". *Landscape and Urban Planning*, 105(3), 221–229.

White, M.P., Alcock, I., Grellier, J., Wheeler, B.W., Hartig, T., et al., (2019). "Spending at least 120 minutes a week in nature is associated with good health and well-being". *Scientific Reports*, 9(1), 7730.

Winterbottom, D. and Wagenfeld, A. (2015). *Therapeutic Gardens: Design for Healing Spaces*, London: Timber Press.

Wood, C.J., Pretty, J., and Griffin, M. (2016). "A case-control study of the health and well-being benefits of allotment gardening". *Journal of Public Health*, 38(3), 336–344.

World Health Organization (2016). "Urban green spaces and health". Copenhagen: WHO Regional Office for Europe.

World Health Organization (2017). "Urban Green Space Intervention and Health. A review of impacts and effectiveness". Copenhagen: WHO Regional Office for Europe.

Organizations

The American Community Gardening Association works to build cohesive communities through gardens. www.communitygarden.org

The American Public Gardens Association offers a wealth of information about gardening for sustainability and well-being. www.publicgardens.org/sustainability-index/attributes/health-well-being

The Chicago Botanic Garden offers a well-respected garden therapy program. www.chicagobotanic.org/therapy

The National Gardening Association has programs to help people get started with all types of home gardening. www.garden.org

The Royal Horticultural Society is a charity that inspires everyone to grow. It wants to enrich everyone's life through plants and make the UK a greener and more beautiful place. For the latest work on health and well-being, visit: rhs.org.uk/well-being

British designer Heather Appleton's Russian Museum Garden features drifts of *Stipa* and *Pennisetum* grasses punctuated with the brilliant crimson of 'Ladybird' poppies for a striking effect.

ABOUT THE AUTHORS

Professor Alistair Griffiths is the RHS Director of Science and Collections. He has a first and a national diploma in horticulture (Myerscough College), a plant science degree and a PhD (University of Reading), and is a fellow of the Chartered Institute of Horticulture and the Royal Society of Biology. He sits on the UK government's Ornamental Horticulture Roundtable Group, and chairs the Health and Horticulture Forum Group. Before his work at the RHS, he was the Eden Project's head scientist. He would like to thank his wife, Nicola Griffiths, for her support during the production of this book.

Matt Keightley is a respected and accomplished multi-award-winning garden designer with more than 16 years' experience in the landscaping industry and a reputation as one of the UK's leading garden designers. He has designed four gardens at the RHS Chelsea Flower Show, achieving four awards, including two for BBC People's Choice for best show garden, first for his Help for Heroes Show Garden in 2014, and for his Hope in Vulnerability Show Garden the year after with HRH Prince Harry, Duke of Sussex, and his charity Sentebale. As well as regularly writing for national publications, he talks at industry events and lectures on garden design. Working closely with the RHS for several years at their flagship garden RHS Garden Wisley, Matt has designed and developed the Well-Being Garden at the entrance of the new National Center for Horticultural Science and Learning.

Annie Gatti is a gardening journalist with a passion for sustainable horticulture. Over the course of her career, she has been an editor for *The Garden Design Journal* and *The Good Gardens Guide*, and commissioning editor of the gardening pages for *The Times*. In 2011, she won the Garden Media Guild Environmental Award for her Eco Watch column in *The English Garden* magazine. Annie currently writes freelance, featuring in a number of leading garden magazines and national newspapers including *The Sunday Times*, *The Telegraph*, and *The Guardian*.

Zia Allaway is a journalist, editor, and qualified horticulturist. She has written a range of gardening books for the RHS and DK including *The Complete Gardeners' Manual*, *How to Grow Practically Everything*, *RHS Practical House Plant Book*, and *Indoor Edible Garden*. She has also worked with Diarmuid Gavin on two of his design books, and edited *The Encyclopedia of Garden Design*. Zia is a contributor to *The Garden Design Journal* and a columnist for *Homes & Gardens* magazine. She runs a consultancy service from her home in Hertfordshire and has a small wildlife garden that she opens to the public through the UK National Gardens Scheme.

RHS SCIENCE TEAM

Since the late 2000s, the RHS Science Team, in collaboration with colleagues from a number of UK, European, and US universities—in particular Sheffield University, Reading University, and Cranfield University—has been looking at the environmental and health benefits and impacts of garden plants, gardening, and gardens.

Our research ranges from studying plant choices for flood resilience to the impacts they have on air quality improvements; understanding biodiversity and the cooling and insulating of buildings; pollution mitigation and the water-holding capacity of soil; and the role of front gardens in promoting human health and well-being. The diversity of our research shows the breadth and impact that gardeners, gardening, and gardens can have upon the environment and the health of the community who use them.

Key areas of research focus on:

Optimizing garden plant diversity for health and environment: RHS Horticultural Taxonomy Team

Health/environmental services of gardens: RHS Environmental Horticulture Team

Changing Climate: RHS Environmental Horticulture Team

Biodiversity and Plant Health: RHS Plant Health Team

Resource use and waste in gardens: RHS Environmental Horticulture Team

Your purchase of this book supports the RHS's charitable works. This work adds to the global knowledge bank of gardening and garden plants that is shared with members and gardeners through the RHS Information and Advice Team on our website; through our schools, publishing program and outreach projects; and via our gardening networks. For more on the RHS Science Strategy and its work visit: www.rhs.org.uk/science

ACKNOWLEDGMENTS

FROM THE PUBLISHER

Dorling Kindersley would like to thank Chris Young at the RHS for having the vision to propose this book concept at RHS Chelsea in 2018; Elena Armenise, groundwater technical advisor, Environment Agency, for her help with soils; Dr. Tijana Blanuša, principal horticultural scientist, RHS, for her help with air pollution and ecosystem services; Helen Bostock, senior horticultural advisor, RHS, for her help with pollinators, predators, wildlife ponds, and meadows; Dr. Ross Cameron and Lauriane Suyin Chalmin-Pui, Sheffield University, for their help on human well-being and landscapes; Professor John W. Dover, Emeritus Professor of Ecology, Staffordshire University, for his help with particulates and air pollution; Dr. Mark Gush, head of environmental horticulture, RHS, for his help with water; Leigh Hunt, principal horticultural advisor, RHS, for his horticultural and ecosystem service advice; Janet Manning, Innovate UK KTP water management specialist, Cranfield University, for her help with water; Dr. Patrick Osborne, Director of Programs for Environmental Science within geography and environmental science, University of Southampton, for his help with noise pollution; Dr. Marc Redmile-Gordon, senior scientist for soil and climate change, RHS, for his help with soils; Dr. Andrew Salisbury, principal entomologist at RHS Garden Wisley, for his help with pollinators and predators.

Jamie Ambrose, Helena Caldon, Joanna Micklem, Jane Simmonds, and Rona Skene for additional writing and editing; John Tullock for additional consulting on the US edition; Sarah Hopper for picture research; Steve Crozier for retouching work; Glenda Fisher, Hannah Moore, Sara Robin, Collette Sadler, and Jessica Tapolcai for additional design; Vanessa Bird for indexing.

Penguin
Random
House

Senior editors Alison Sturgeon, Dawn Titmus
Senior designer Barbara Zuniga
Editor Toby Mann
US editor Karyn Gerhard
Project art editor Harriet Yeomans
Designer Mandy Earey
Editorial assistant Millie Andrew
Illustrators Keith Hagan, Nicola Powling
Senior jacket designer Nicola Powling
Jacket coordinator Lucy Philpott
Pre-production producer David Almond
Senior producer Stephanie McConnell
Managing editor Stephanie Farrow
Managing art editor Christine Keilty
Art director Maxine Pedliham
Publishing director Mary-Clare Jerram

First American Edition, 2020
Published in the United States by DK Publishing
1450 Broadway, Suite 801, New York, NY 10018

Copyright © 2020 Dorling Kindersley Limited
DK, a Division of Penguin Random House LLC
20 21 22 23 24   10 9 8 7 6 5 4 3 2 1
001–314641–Feb/2020

A catalog record for this book is available from the Library of Congress.
ISBN: 978-1-4654-8959-3

DK books are available at special discounts when purchased in bulk for sales
promotions, fund-raising, or educational use. For details, contact:
DK Publishing Special Markets, 1450 Broadway, Suite 801,
New York, NY 10018 or SpecialSales@dk.com

Printed and bound in Canada

A WORLD OF IDEAS:
SEE ALL THERE IS TO KNOW

www.dk.com

DISCLAIMER

The information in this book has been compiled as general guidance
on the specific subjects addressed, and some of the plants shown
or described may be harmful or are poisonous to ingest. The
information in this book is not a substitute and not to be relied on for
medical, healthcare, or pharmaceutical professional advice. Please
consult your physician before changing, stopping, or starting any
medical treatment or using any plant-based remedies. As far as the
authors are aware, the information given is correct and up-to-date
as of November 22, 2019. Practice, laws, and regulations all change,
and the reader should obtain up-to-date professional advice on any
such issues. The author and publishers disclaim, as far as the law
allows, any liability arising directly or indirectly from the use or misuse
of the information contained in this book.